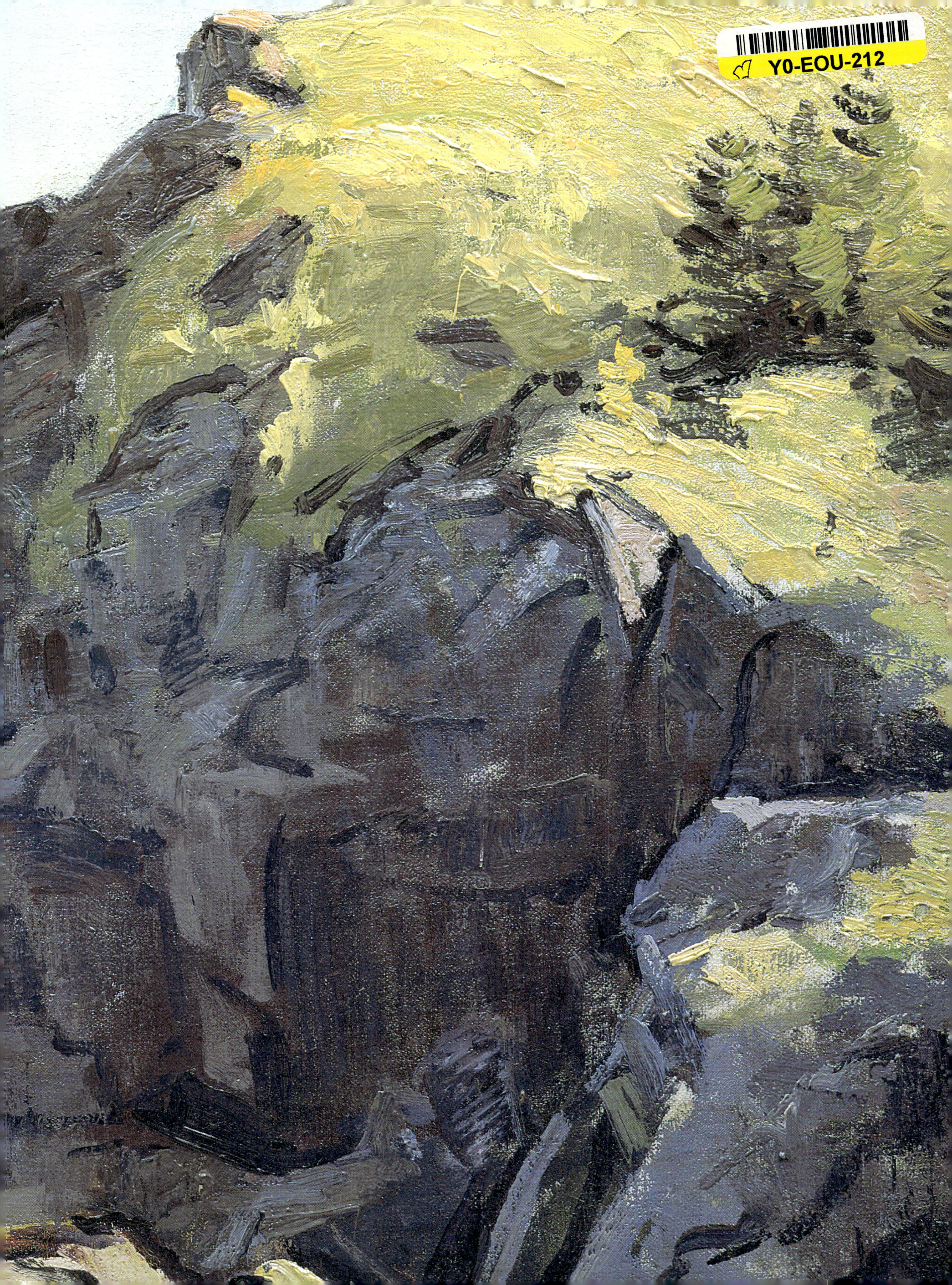

they have not really hurt the wild effect of the island except in the village part they have not added to its character or its beauty.

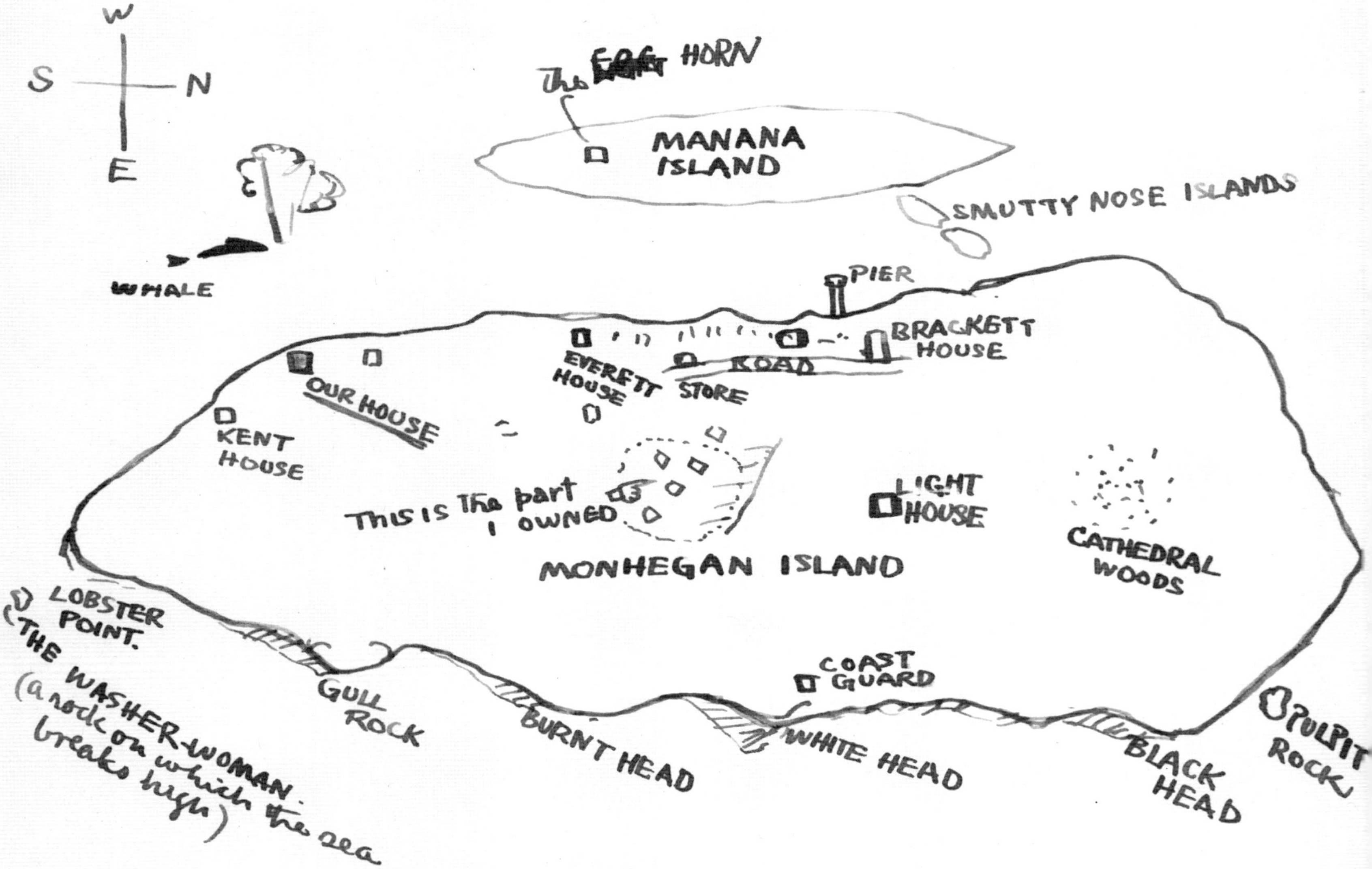

This is by no means a correct map but it will serve to recall to you the island and the lay of the land and will show you where our house is — note the red spot. —

We met Everett last night. He does not seem much older. looks very much the same altho quite gray — white. He is the same enthusiast about art. is now the

Abraham J. Bogdanove

(1886–1946)

Painter of Maine

Map of Monhegan, Maine, September 3, 1918, Robert Henri Papers, The Yale Collection of American Literature, Beineke Rare Book and Manuscript Library, Yale University, New Haven, Connecticut.

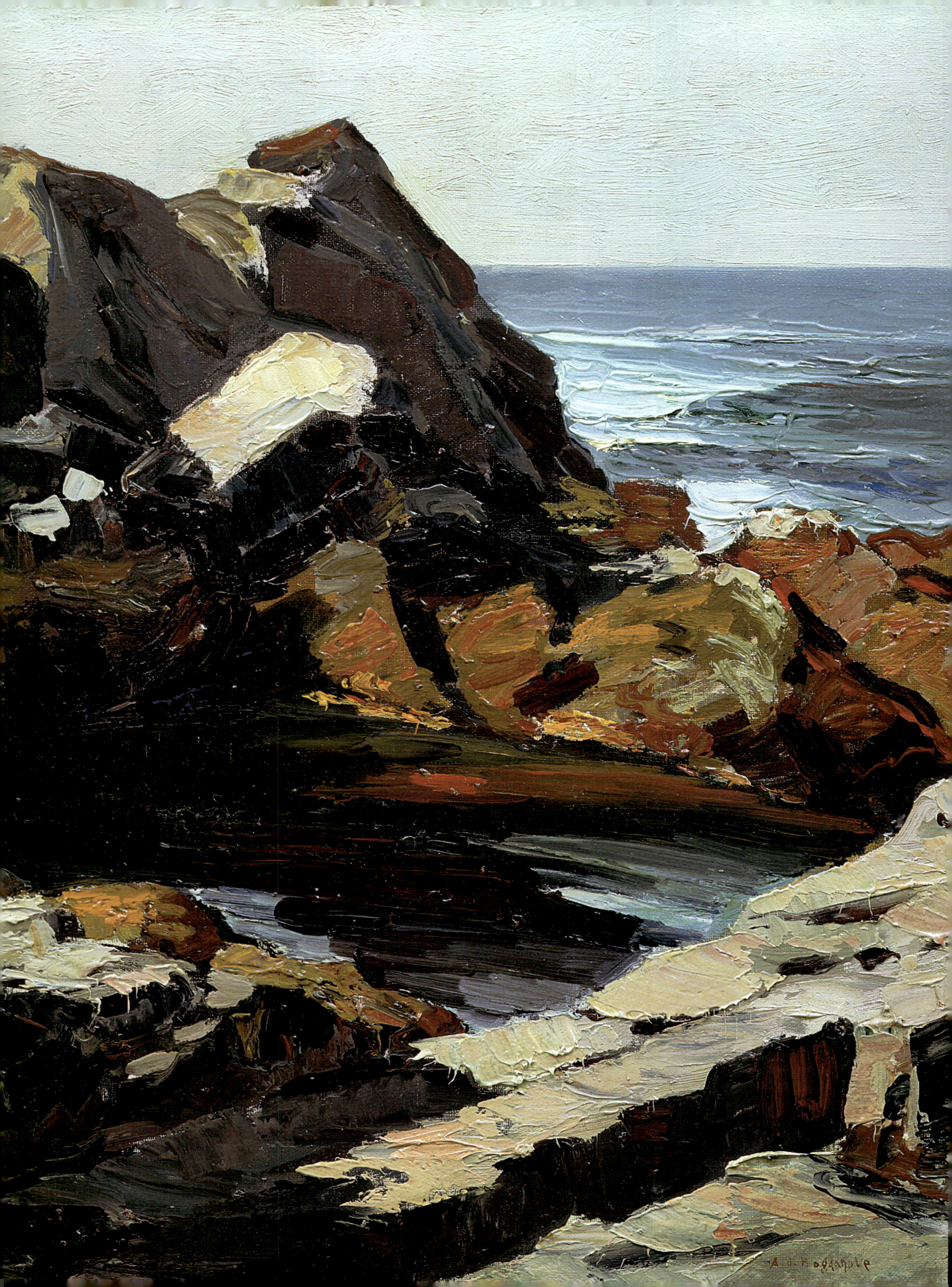
A. J. Bogdanove

Abraham J. Bogdanove

(1886–1946)

Painter of Maine

by Jessica Nicoll

Spanierman Gallery, LLC

45 East 58th Street New York, NY 10022 Telephone (212) 832-0208 Fax (212) 832-8114 http://www.spanierman.com

Published in the United States of America in 1997 by
Spanierman Gallery, LLC, 45 East 58th Street, New York, NY 10022

ISBN 0-945936-15-X

Design: Marcus Ratliff
Composition: Amy Pyle
Imagesetting: Center Page
Lithography: Meridian Printing

Acknowledgments

AT THE OUTSET of this project, Abraham Bogdanove was, for me, an enigmatic figure among the hundreds of artists who have traveled to Maine's remote Monhegan Island during the past century. Little seemed to be known about him personally, but the body of work that he left behind revealed an artist of intelligence and gusto and provoked curiosity about his career. With his art as a point of entry, Bogdanove's life gradually came into focus through a patchwork of academic records, exhibition catalogues and reviews, personal recollections, and decades of newspaper clippings. The man that emerged was as vital and intriguing as his paintings, and his story illuminates a sparsely documented chapter in Monhegan's evolution as an artists' colony.

I am grateful to Ira Spanierman and Spanierman Gallery, LLC, New York, for entrusting me with the recovery of Bogdanove's history. Special thanks are due to Deborah Gerstler Spanierman, associate director, for her patience and support throughout this process, and to Lisa N. Peters, director of research, for helping me keep my facts straight and true.

In many ways, this has been a group effort, and I am indebted to the individuals and institutions who assisted my research. Thanks go to members of the Bogdanove family for their unstinting generosity in sharing information from the impressive archive they have compiled. The residents of Monhegan's art community were also invaluable sources, notably Ed Deci and Beth Van Houten of the Monhegan Museum; Bill Boynton of the Lupine Gallery; and Jackie Hudson and Clara McPherson Reiss. Finally, thanks are due to the many archivists, librarians, and curators who responded to my inquiries, particularly the staff of the Archives of American Art, Smithsonian Institution, New York and Washington, D.C. and David Dearinger, associate curator and archivist at the National Academy of Design.

Jessica Nicoll

Jessica Nicoll, chief curator at the Portland Museum of Art, Maine, earned her undergraduate degree in art history and American studies from Smith College and her M.A. from the Winterthur Program in Early American Culture at the University of Delaware. Formerly curator of exhibits at Old Sturbridge Village, she has organized numerous exhibitions including *Meet Your Neighbors: Portraits, Painters, and Society in Rural New England, 1790–1850,* held at Old Sturbridge Village in 1992 and *The Allure of the Maine Coast: Robert Henri and His Circle, 1903–1918,* held at The Portland Museum of Art, Maine, in 1995, and has lectured on a variety of topics in the field of American art.

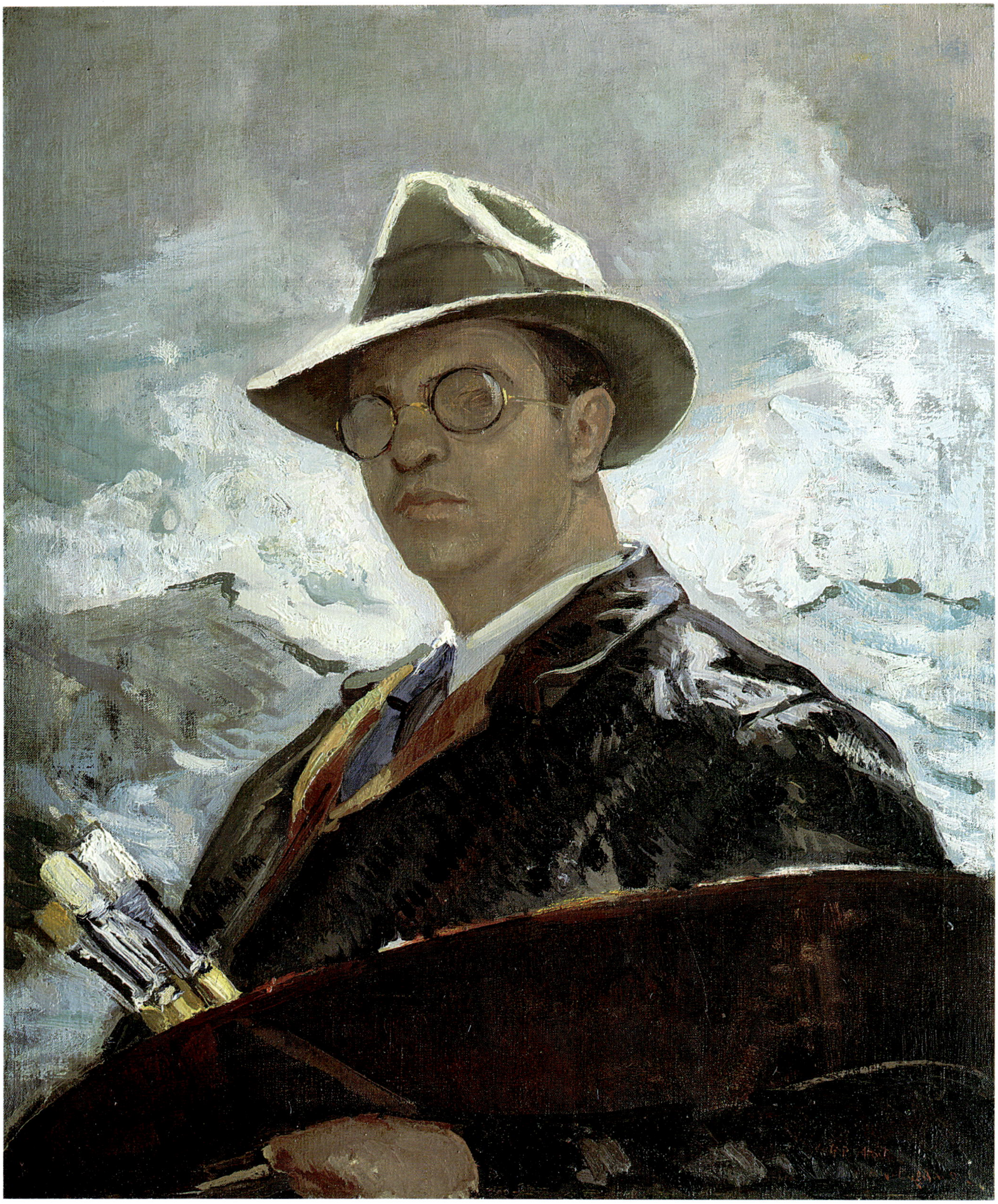

Fig. 1. Abraham Bogdanove. *Self-portrait,* ca. 1935–1942, oil on canvas, 30 × 25 in. (76.2 × 63.5 cm).

Abraham J. Bogdanove (1886–1946): Painter of Maine

At the height of his career in the late 1930s, Abraham Bogdanove painted a self-portrait that offers an incisive glimpse of its creator (fig. 1). He often turned his eye on himself, like many painters in search of a ready model, but where his other efforts were mere likenesses, this *Self-portrait* proclaimed his artistic identity.[1] He depicted himself confronting the viewer directly, creating an emblem of his alliance with traditional artists' self-portraits and academic paintings. The portrayal conveys Bogdanove's physical power and energy by framing his head and upper torso against a turbulent sea crashing over gray rocks. The painting clearly does not depict the artist in his studio. Bogdanove's jaunty, brimmed hat and overcoat indicate that he is out of doors, a chronicler of the sea, painting from direct experience.

Self-portrait makes the important distinction that Bogdanove's identity as a marine painter took precedence over his roles as portraitist, muralist, and teacher. Those activities filled his time during the academic year in New York City and provided a stable livelihood, but he invested his greatest creative energy and autonomy in the paintings he made during summers on Maine's Monhegan Island. His *Self-portrait* clearly identifies the work by which he wanted to be known and remembered. It is a bold public statement directed to his peers—both comrades and competitors—in New York. New York was where Bogdanove first realized his ambition to be an artist, where he studied, and where he fought for recognition, but Maine provided him with his muse.

Bogdanove had lived in New York City since 1900, when, at the age of thirteen, he emigrated with his family from Minsk, Russia. The Bogdanoves were part of the large wave of Russian Jewish immigrants who came to America at the turn of the century. Soon after settling in New York, Abraham began studying art at the Cooper Union Institute of Art. In 1903, he entered the National Academy of Design school and, at the same time, served an apprenticeship, painting advertisement displays for the Bull Durham Company in New York. Through this dual education, Bogdanove developed his abilities in design, draftsmanship, and painting. His studies at the academy were directed by the painters George Willoughby Maynard (1843–1923) and Francis Coates Jones (1857–1932), and by the end of his tenure in 1911, he had earned several honors. For three consecutive years, he received the distinguished annual Hallgarten Prize, which was bestowed upon the three best paintings exhibited at the academy by artists under the age of thirty-five.[2]

Bogdanove rounded out his education with two years at the Columbia University School of Architecture (1908–1910). Like Rockwell Kent (1882–1971) before him, his studies there sharpened his abilities as a designer and gave him commercially useful skills. His decision to enroll at Columbia may have been guided by his ambition to be a muralist. He was a studio assistant to Francis Millet (1846–1912), one of the leading mural painters in the country, and it is likely that Millet advised him that the study of architecture would be beneficial.[3]

At the conclusion of his formal education, Bogdanove followed in the footsteps of many artists with a pilgrimage to Europe, arriving in Italy in 1912. Later in life he recalled departing with a sketchbook, a knapsack, and a hundred dollars; "My chum went with me. He had a job on the boat. By good luck, the captain let me work my passage as cabin boy and I landed on a seaman's pass. We didn't hurry back. We had come to see the country."[4] Bogdanove traveled to Germany, Austria, and France, and eventually returned to Italy where he bribed a concierge for a small space that he converted to a studio.

On his return from Europe in the following year, Bogdanove received his first mural commission to create a frieze on the themes of shelter and nurture for the Hebrew Sheltering and Guardian Society, a home for children in Pleasantville, New York. Bogdanove's study of painting and architecture had sufficiently equipped him to conceive and execute a large-scale design successfully unified with its architectural setting. It also earned him a New York City Board of Education license, as a specialist in art mural decoration, and a position teaching at the New York Evening School of Industrial Art.

Other murals soon followed as the artist won commissions for works in civic buildings in New York City. These opportunities arose from the new interest in murals that flourished in the United States beginning at the turn of the century. Prior to that time, there had been no established American tradition of mural painting. The first real efforts in the genre were stimulated by commissions from Charles McKim (1847–1909), of the architectural firm McKim, Mead & White, for several large public projects. McKim employed Pierre Puvis de Chavannes (1824–1898), John Singer Sargent (1856–1925), and Edwin Austin Abbey (1852–1911) to create murals for the Boston Public Library (1890–1919) and conceived an ambitious mural project for the Chicago Columbian Exposition in 1893, which was executed by an army of artists, including Kenyon Cox (1856–1919) and J. Alden Weir (1852–1919). The Chicago project exerted a tremendous and immediate influence, spawning painted decorations in state capitols, courthouses, government buildings, and libraries throughout the country.

Millet, Bogdanove's mentor, was an integral part of this movement. He was a member of a circle of artists who were friendly with McKim and Stanford White (1853–1906), including Sargent, Abbey, John La Farge (1835–1910), Augustus Saint-Gaudens (1848–1907), George de Forest Brush (1855–1941), and William Merritt Chase (1849–1916). Millet painted murals from Cleveland to Cambridge, and was La Farge's collaborator on the decorations for Trinity Church in Boston. As Millet's studio assistant, Bogdanove gained entry to this world. Sadly, his first solo commission came in 1912, the year that Millet was lost on the Titanic.

Bogdanove's murals, like most of the murals of this period, were informed by Renaissance models. They all addressed historical, educational, or moral themes and were usually composed symmetrically, with one dominant figure providing a strong central axis. Bogdanove was praised for developing his ideas simply and graphically so that they could be comprehended quickly by passing viewers. He did not use the traditional technique of painting on plaster, but instead employed the modern method of painting on canvas, which allowed him to work in a studio and then install the mural on site when it was completed.

The success of Bogdanove's second mural project, two paintings contrasting ancient and modern commerce for Brooklyn's Commercial High School, led to subsequent commissions for edifying art works for New York City schools. These included a three-part mural on the theme of education for Commercial High School, and three paintings illustrating the European discovery and colonization of North America for P.S. 43 in the Bronx. One of Bogdanove's most successful public works was a nineteen-by-fifteen-foot painting, *Peace*, for the main stairway in Brooklyn's Manual Training High School. A memorial to the twenty-five graduates of the high school who had died during World War I, the subject must have had particular resonance for an artist who had been "in the first class of the drafted men."[5] The mural was praised publicly for its depiction of "a soldier telling the future generations of what he fought for in the war and . . . four figures beating the swords of war into ploughshares of peace. Above . . . these figures is seen the figure of peace holding aloft the light of understanding and the olive branch of peace."[6] Bogdanove's last major commission was a mural entitled *The Great Teachers*, completed in 1930 for the College of the City of New York (now City College, The City University of New York), where he taught from 1919 to 1942.[7]

As his aspirations as a muralist were realized, Bogdanove increasingly devoted his free time, particularly the summers, to painting for himself. His early paintings, such as *The Wanderer* (ca. 1920; location unknown) and *The Guide to the Perplexed* (ca. 1920; location unknown), were consistent with his mural work, demonstrating academic styles and didactic messages. But by the 1910s, Bogdanove had made his first forays into landscape painting, with trips to the countrysides of Connecticut and New Jersey. The loose, impressionistic brushwork of paintings like *Creek Woods, Connecticut* (pl. 15) show the artist pushing himself to develop a style distinct from the crisp, classical rendering at which he excelled in his murals.

This new direction in his art was quickly followed by a shift in his public exhibition venues and the paintings he showed. Whereas in 1913 he entered mural studies in the annual exhibition of the Architectural League of New York, in 1916 he had a landscape painting accepted to the annual exhibition at the National Academy of Design.[8] In so doing, he went from being known primarily as a designer and decorator to being recognized by his peers as a serious creative artist. In 1920, Bogdanove had his first solo exhibition of twenty-seven paintings.[9] While the checklist included *The Guide to the Perplexed* and a sketch for a mural, fully twenty of the paintings were land- or seascapes. Of those, the majority were views of Maine's Monhegan Island, signaling a crucial new chapter in the artist's life.

Bogdanove first visited Maine in the summer of 1915, when he stayed at Seal Harbor on Mount Desert Island. The island's dramatic vistas of mountains plunging to the sea must have been as inspiring to Bogdanove as they had been to Frederic Church (1826–1900) and Fitz Hugh Lane (1804–1865), for he returned the following two summers. Equally alluring was the social world into which he was introduced by his friend Clara Clemens, the daughter of Mark Twain. At the afternoon teas she hosted, he made the acquaintance of John D. Rockefeller and the actor John Barrymore, among others. To Bogdanove, these opportunities were worth the suffering of wearing "a stiff collar and taking part in the light chit-chat."[10]

By 1918, the refinements of summer life on Mount Desert had lost their attraction, and Bogdanove went in search of rougher locales. He found his way to Monhegan, a tiny island seventeen miles off the mid-coast of Maine, where stiff collars and formal teas were unknown. Instead of mountainous scenery, Monhegan offered a compact and varied landscape, unique among the hundreds of islands that dot Maine's coastal waters. Less than two miles long and a mile wide, the island includes a picturesque harbor lined with fish houses, rolling meadows, pine woods, and cliffs soaring two hundred feet above the open ocean. For an artist it is paradise, remote and quiet, with an inspiring range of subjects. Robert Henri (1865–1929), one of the first New York painters to visit Monhegan, summed up the reaction of most artists when he enthused in 1903:

> This is the real thing, I have never seen anything so fine.... from the great cliffs you look down on a mighty surf battering away at the rocks ... and then you can disappear from the sea into the pine forrests [sic]–they are wild. The village is on the inland side–a little harbor shielded by a small island–simply a huge mass of rock. It is a wonderful place to paint–so much in so small a place one can hardly believe it. I am already wondering if it may not be possible to have a summer studio here.[11]

Like Henri, Bogdanove found in Monhegan a subject worthy of sustained focus. After a captivating first encounter, he returned every summer for the rest of his life.

Bogdanove would have been well aware of Monhegan's possibilities long before he experienced them, for the island already had a reputation among artists. The Boston-based painters Eric Hudson (1864–1932) and Samuel Triscott (1846–1925) had both found Monhegan in the late nineteenth century and were among the first artists to build homes and studios there. Beginning in 1903, a contingent of New York painters, led by Henri, claimed Monhegan as a foil to more accessible, and tamer, summer resorts like Gloucester, Massachusetts, and Ogunquit, Maine. Henri's enthusiasm for the island prompted several of his most promising students, including Rockwell Kent and George Bellows (1882–1925), to follow him there. The canvases that Kent painted on Monhegan between 1905 and 1907 established his reputation, causing John Sloan (1871–1951) to proclaim, "These pictures are immense Rocks and Sea.... Splendid big thoughts. Some like big prayers to God. I enjoyed them to the utmost and accept them as great."[12] The exhibition in New York of those and other Monhegan paintings introduced still more artists to the island, and inspired them to visit. The years leading up to World War I saw increasing numbers of painters mingling in the summertime with Monhegan's year-round community of fishermen and their families.

Bogdanove would have had ample opportunity to see works by these artists in New York. They were regularly featured in exhibitions organized by Henri and his circle at the MacDowell Club, where Bogdanove exhibited in 1918.[13] The National Academy of Design's annual exhibitions often included selections from productive summer stays in Maine and on Monhegan. For example, after his first visit to Monhegan in 1911, Frederick Judd Waugh (1861–1940) entered *Coast of Monhegan* in that year's winter exhibition. During the next few years, Waugh showed canvases from subsequent stays on the island, including *Black Head in Fog, Near Lobster Cove: Monhegan,* and *Off the Coast of Maine.*[14] All of these were subjects that Bogdanove would himself paint within a decade.

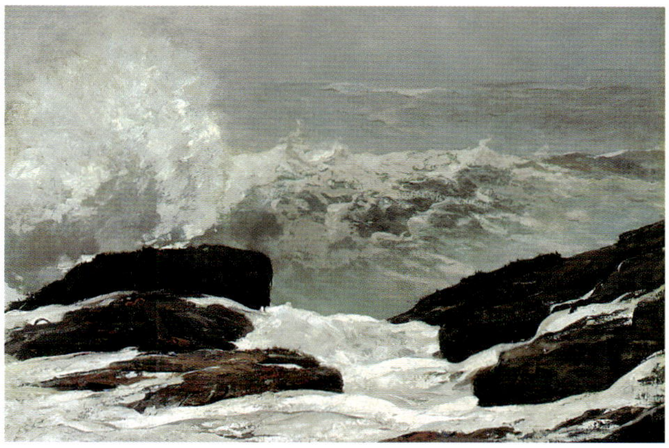

Fig. 2. Winslow Homer, *Maine Coast,* 1896, oil on canvas, 30 × 40 in. (76.2 × 101.6 cm), The Metropolitan Museum of Art, Gift of George A. Hearn, in memory of Arthur Hoppock Hearn, 1911, 11.116.1. Photograph © 1989 The Metropolitan Museum of Art.

The National Academy of Design was the locus of a renaissance in marine painting at this time. Howard Russell Butler (1856–1934), Paul Dougherty (1877–1947) (a Henri student and a frequent visitor to Monhegan), William Ritschel (1864–1949), and Waugh were among the painters building reputations on dramatic and realistic depictions of the Atlantic and were all affiliated with the academy while Bogdanove was studying there. A prime catalyst for this interest in marine painting was the work of Winslow Homer (1836–1910). In the early years of the century, several of Homer's late, great paintings of surf-beaten rocks at Prout's Neck, Maine, had been exhibited at the academy to stirring effect. Henri was among those who credited Homer's works with inspiring him to try to capture the terrible beauty of the sea, to create "an integrity of nature."[15]

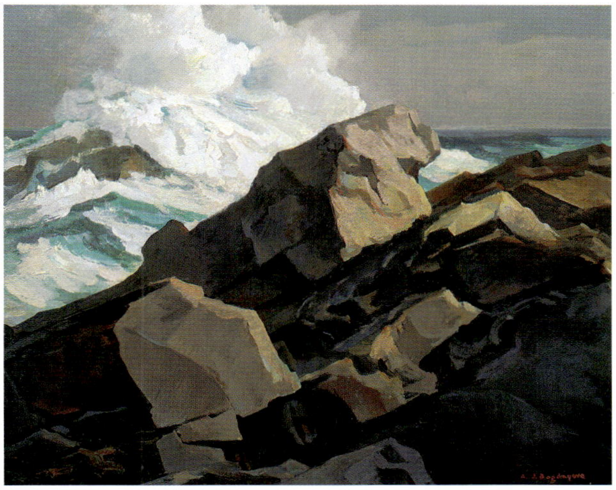

Fig. 3. Abraham Bogdanove, *Low Tide Surf,* ca. 1940, oil on panel, 30 × 36 in. (76.2 × 91.4 cm).

In the 1890s, Homer's compressed images of rocks and sea had transformed the notion of the seascape. Gone were such narrative devices as ships in peril or men resisting the pull of surf. The devastating power of the sea was more potently expressed by Homer's evocation of wrathful waves assaulting leaden rocks. It is evident in Bogdanove's surf paintings that he had studied, and learned the lessons of, such Homer masterpieces as *Maine Coast* (fig. 2). In related pictures like *Low Tide Surf* (fig. 3), Bogdanove used Homer's strategy of conveying the force of the sea and the resistance of the rock by positioning the viewer at a low vantage point behind the rocks, directly confronting a crashing wave. Unlike a broader or more distant view of the coast, the immediacy and power of this composition focuses on the opposition of forces, creating a potent metaphor for man's battle with nature. It also shows Bogdanove applying the advice that his academy classmate Leon Kroll (1884–1974) had received from Homer: "If you want to do a great sea, use only two waves."[16]

A posthumous exhibition catalogue makes the intriguing claim that Bogdanove first visited Monhegan in the company of Waugh.[17] The latter had frequented the island between 1911 and 1914, and in 1916 he published a children's fantasy, *The Clan of the Munes,* inspired by the mysterious Cathedral Woods, but there is no firm evidence that Waugh traveled to

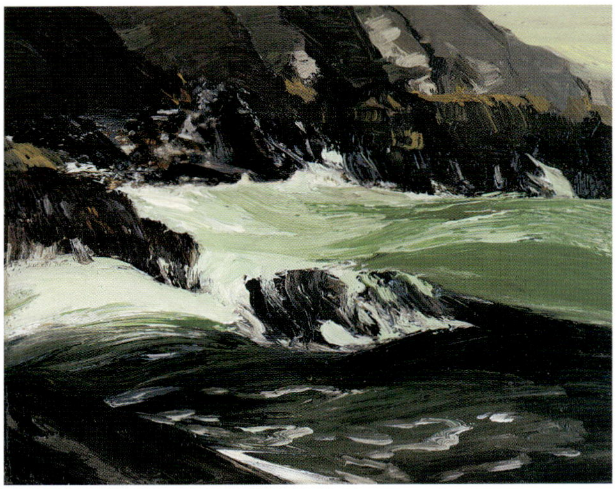

Fig. 4. Robert Henri, *Rocks and Sea*, 1905, oil on canvas, 11½ × 15 in. (29.2 × 38.1 cm), Portland Museum of Art, Maine, Bequest of Elizabeth B. Noyce.

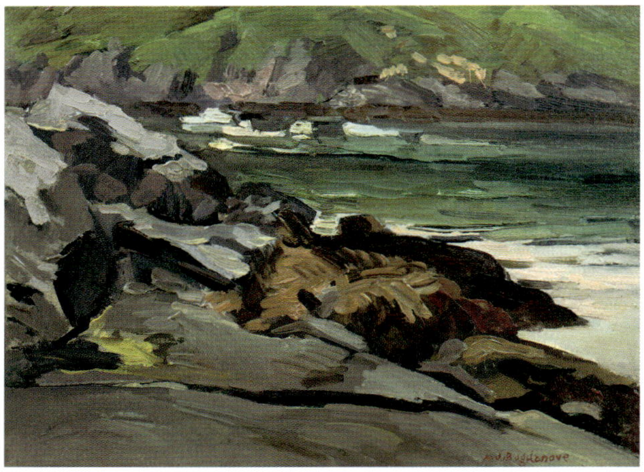

Fig. 5. Abraham Bogdanove, *Oceanside*, ca. 1925–1935, oil on canvasboard, 12 × 16 in. (30.5 × 40.6 cm).

Maine in 1918. However, this does suggest a more personal connection between Bogdanove and an artist who was at the forefront of American marine painting. Bogdanove's 1934 application for membership in the Salmagundi Club confirms that the two were acquainted—the artists who proposed Bogdanove for membership identified Waugh as among the members who knew him. It is plausible that Waugh was either directly or indirectly responsible for Bogdanove's desire to experience Monhegan firsthand.

The island that Bogdanove visited in 1918 was very different from the bustling artists' colony populated by Bellows, Waugh, Dougherty, and others just a few years earlier. With the United States's entry into World War I, the tiny and remote island suddenly seemed frighteningly vulnerable and most artists stayed away. One of the few to visit that fall was Henri, back after an absence of seven years. He found the island transformed by war, with the lighthouse surrounded by a secured enclosure and patrol boats sailing in the waters offshore. As he wrote to his brother: "The war while it killed off half of Monhegan's little quota of summer visitors has quite put the island on the map. Yesterday a man-of-war plowed by accompanied with two smaller war vessels . . . they came almost within hailing distance of us, looked formidable with their guns and their speed."[18] Edward Hopper (1882–1967) was also on the island that summer, returning for his third visit with his friend, artist Clarence Chatterton (1880–1973). Hopper seemed to enjoy the relative quiet that war had brought. As he told a local newspaper, "Maine is so beautiful and the weather is so fine in the summer—that's why I come here to rest and to paint a little, too."[19]

Bogdanove had similar reasons for settling on Monhegan. During his eighteenth season on the island he reflected:

> There are a number of reasons why I prefer Monhegan to all other places on the Atlantic Coast. It is so far from the mainland that we are not disturbed by the outer world and there are no social demands. The cliffs here are so bold and precipitous and the studies offered by the island shore so inexhaustible. The climate suits me. Perhaps because it is more like that of Russia, where my ancestors lived.[20]

Within two years of his first visit, Bogdanove had purchased a house, making a lifetime commitment to the island. He was part of a new generation of painters, including Andrew Winter (1893–1958) and Jay Hall Connaway (1893–1970), who came to Monhegan and stayed. The prewar colony had been characterized by a constantly changing roster of artists who alternated visits to Monhegan with stays at Gloucester, Massachusetts, and such Maine coastal towns as Ogunquit. The artists working on the island in the 1920s and 1930s created a more sustained sense of community, often staying there in all seasons of the year. The body of work produced over several decades by these painters reflected a new depth of experience.

The house Bogdanove purchased in 1920 was situated on Horn's Hill, an area overlooking the village that was developed early in the century, concurrent with the first influx of artists on the island. "George Everett [1865–1926], the artist turned speculator in real estate ... had bought Horn's Hill, had made a pretty map of it with building lots and rights of way."[21] Henri had owned a plot of land there, but never realized his hope of constructing a studio, unlike Kent, who had used his carpentry skills to build a house and studio. Bogdanove's property also had an Everett lineage; when he purchased the house, he was told that it had been Randall Davey's (1887–1964) studio when he was on Monhegan with Bellows in the early 1910s.[22] The small cottage, which still stands, is dominated by a large, central studio off of which are two small bedrooms, a kitchen, and a porch. It is a short hike to the headlands, and the north-facing studio window offers a prospect stretching from the hilltop lighthouse across open meadows to the harbor. The view from the porch is captured in Bogdanove's *Portrait of Mrs. "W." (The Artist's Wife)* (pl. 20), a painting of the artist's wife, Pearl Winton, perched on the railing, with the entrance to the harbor behind her.

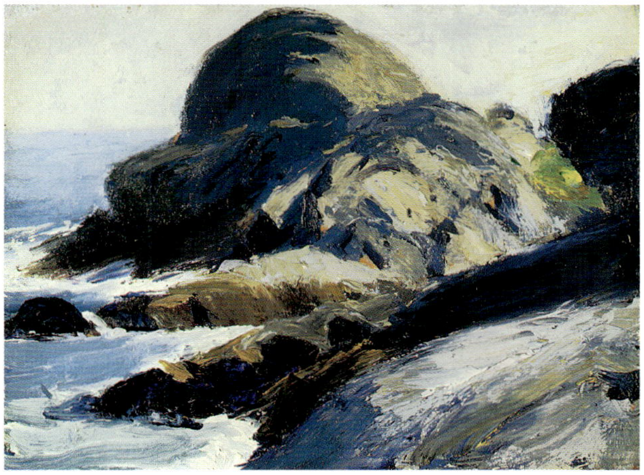

Fig. 6. Edward Hopper, *Rocky Shore*, 1916–1919, oil on wood, 9½ × 13 in. (24.1 × 33 cm), Whitney Museum of American Art, New York, Josephine N. Hopper Bequest, 70.1309. Photograph copyright © 1997 Whitney Museum of American Art.

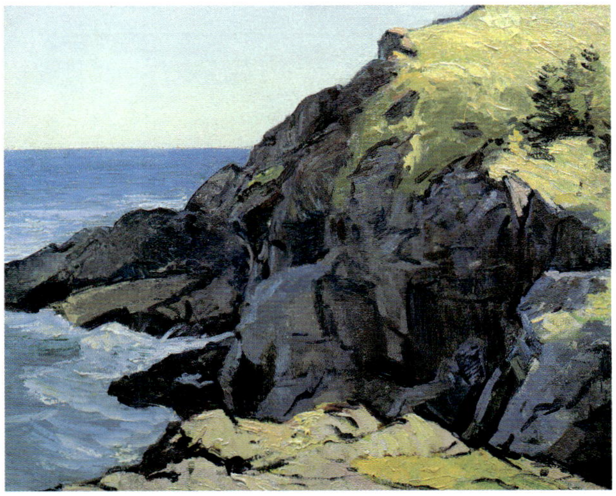

Fig. 7. Abraham Bogdanove, *Monhegan Coast*, ca. 1930–1940, oil on canvas, 25⅛ × 30 in. (63.8 × 76.2 cm).

During the summers, Bogdanove's preference was not to paint in the studio. As he told an interviewer, "If I have to do anything indoors it's just too bad." He went on to describe a disciplined daily routine of "rising as early in midsummer as 3:00 a.m. to take advantage of the early morning light, and working steadily until 11:00 a.m."[23] Painting directly from nature is a tradition on Monhegan, but also a challenge. The terrain is rough and hilly, with a limited system of rutted dirt roads and a network of narrow deer trails leading to the cliffs and rocky shorelines. Like most painters on the island, Bogdanove devised a streamlined kit—a paintbox that doubled as an easel, carried by a shoulder strap—to make hiking easier. Residents still remember seeing "Bog" or "Bogy" almost daily, painting views of the harbor, seated or standing directly on the rocks, with a pipe clamped in his teeth.

Bogdanove used the same working methods as had Robert Henri on his visits to Monhegan, with similar results. Henri traveled with a pochade box—a paint box with panels fitted in the lid for quick sketching—bringing on each trip to the island upwards of ten dozen small wooden panels supplied by Nathan Rabinowitz, a New York purveyor of artist's materials whom Bogdanove also patronized. In the space of four weeks, Henri would cover all of the panels with paint and, when he exhausted his supply, start painting on the backs of them. These small works, like *Rocks and Sea* (fig. 4), each record an intense impression of a specific moment. Henri executed them rapidly, usually in under an hour, and directly, applying the paint in saturated strokes of pure color without the aid of under-

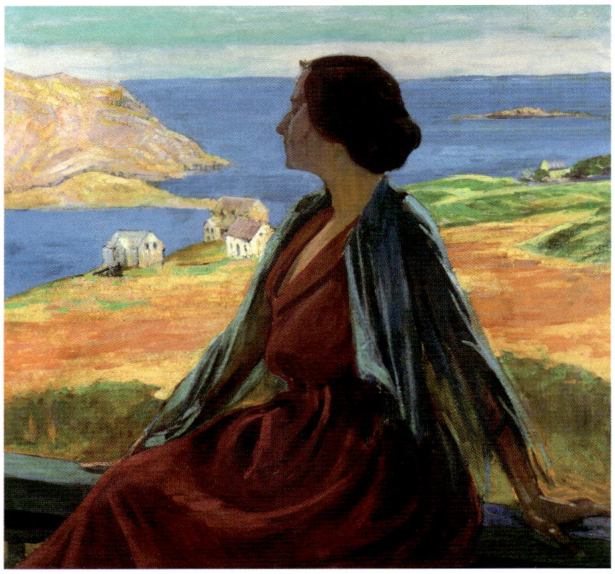

Fig. 8. Abraham Bogdanove, *Portrait of Mrs. W* (*The Artist's Wife*), ca. 1920, oil on canvas, 36 × 38 in. (91.4 × 96.5 cm).

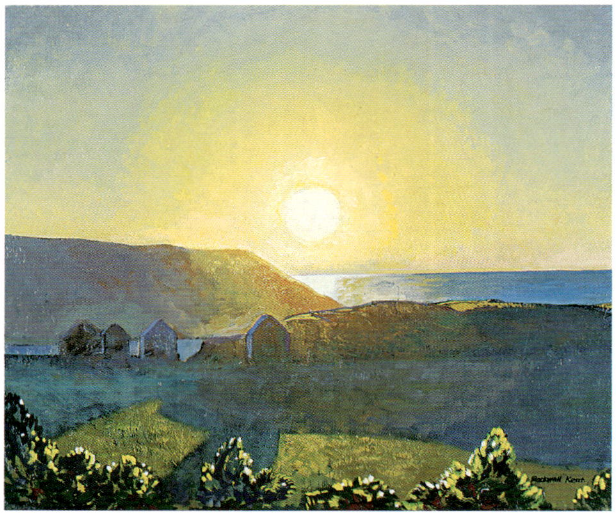

Fig. 9. Rockwell Kent, *Sun, Manana, Monhegan*, 1907, oil on canvas, 20 × 24 in. (50.8 × 61 cm), Bowdoin College Museum of Art, Brunswick, Maine.

drawing. Bogdanove's jewel-like miniatures, like *Oceanside* (fig. 5), have a comparable immediacy. Neither artists' pochades fit the traditional definition of a quick, rough sketch to be developed later. Both saw them as finished works, intended to evoke for the viewer a direct experience of nature.

Bogdanove was particularly drawn to the shore, whether it was to the boats and fish houses along the harbor, the breakers at Lobster Cove, or the headlands towering above the ocean. He saw Monhegan as a place for marine subjects, ignoring the island's fields and forests. Perhaps even more than the ocean, he delighted in painting rocks; he was more attracted to their mass than he was to the movement of the water. He had this in common with Hopper, whose time on Monhegan was spent painting small studies of massive rock formations. Works like Hopper's *Rocky Shore* (fig. 6) and Bogdanove's *Monhegan Coast* (fig. 7), share a focus on the solidity and monumentality of the rocks that anchor the island. Both artists depicted them in a rich variety of colors, ranging from the predictable gray to brown, ochre, red, and blue. Bogdanove claimed that the rainbow hues of the rocks were what held his interest. When challenged by the assertion that the rocks were gray, he explained, the colors "are there if one can see them, it all depends on how the artist sees color. The eye can be trained but there is not much hope for a painter unless he has a natural eye for the finer shadings and harmonies.... Nature never makes mistakes in color harmony."[24]

Bogdanove's approach to color and form reflected an awareness of the work of his predecessors. The vivid color of *Portrait of Mrs. W. (The Artist's Wife)* (fig. 8) can be seen in earlier works by Kent, like *Sun, Manana, Monhegan* (fig. 9). The almost surreal intensity of the color in both of these paintings expresses the quality of light when the sun sets behind Manana, the small island that shelters Monhegan's harbor. Dramatically backlit, Manana and the fish houses are transformed into geometric masses. The abstracted forms in Bogdanove's painting suggest a familiarity with Kent's work—the crisp, flattened shapes that Kent first experimented with in his early works would become a hallmark of his style.

While Bogdanove's use of vibrant yellows, oranges, and blues evokes Kent's style, the dominance of bright green and purple-gray in works like *Fish Houses, Monhegan* (fig. 10) is closer to Bellows's Monhegan paintings. From 1913 on, Bellows was preoccupied with the application of different color theories. One, in particular emphasized the use of a restricted palette, drawn from the spectrum between two complementary colors. The range from green through gray to purple was a favorite for Bellows, which he used in many of his landscapes and marine views. The freshness and apparent spontaneity of paintings like *Hill and Valley, Monhegan, Maine* (fig. 11) belie their theoretical underpinnings.

Application of color theory was a continual focus of Bogdanove's work on Monhegan. He employed the principles of Maximilian Toch, a color theorist and chemist, who advocated the use of natural pigments and a limited palette—in opposition to the profusion of premixed colors in hundreds of shades, and the accompanying color theories, then flooding the art market. Toch's methodology had the goals of creating a more harmonious palette and paintings that were "permanent," that would not discolor or disintegrate because of poor chemistry. There is evidence that Bogdanove worked for Toch earlier in his career, learning lessons that he would apply throughout his life. Toch repaid the favor by publicly praising the artist's work:

> A. J. Bogdanove is not only an excellent painter but he has an intuitive sense of light, shade and third dimension. . . . Frequently he strikes a dramatic note which reminds one of Winslow Homer and Frederick Waugh. . . .In the painting of the rocky foreground on some of his Maine pictures you can almost walk around the rocks and feel the swirling of the green water.[25]

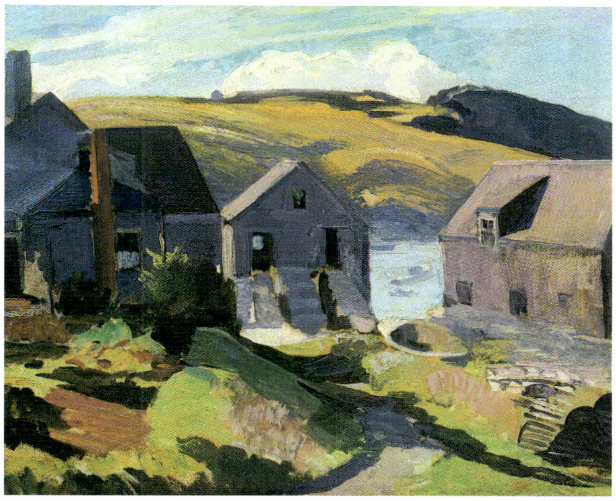

Fig. 10. Abraham Bogdanove, *Fish Houses, Monhegan,* ca. 1925–1935, oil on canvas, (76.2 × 91.4 cm). Private collection, Connecticut.

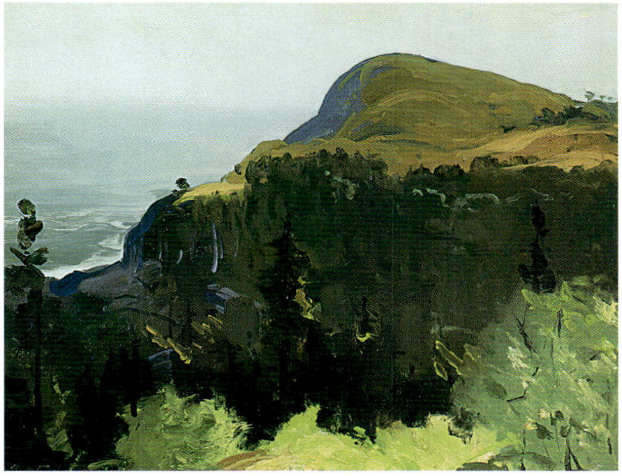

Fig. 11. George Bellows, *Hill and Valley, Monhegan, Maine,* 1913, oil on panel, 16 × 20 in. (40.6 × 50.8 cm), Colby College Museum of Art, Waterville, Maine.

Although Monhegan's primary inspiration for Bogdanove was its landscape, he also derived sustenance from the community of resident artists. Hudson was the senior artist on the island in those years, and his house on the edge of the harbor became a meeting place for nightly dialogue and critique. Hudson's daughter Jackie recalls "how as a young child her presence was frequently overlooked and she sat on the floor and listened to the vehement discussions carried on in front of the blazing fire by a cluster of her father's artist friends. . . . such painters as George Bellows, Randall Davey, Robert Henri, Frederick J. Waugh, Sears Gallagher [1869–1955], Warren P. Lombard [1855–1939], Charles Hovey Pepper [1864–1950], Theophile Schneider [b. 1872], and A. J. Bogdanove."[26]

This dialogue carried over into the work of the artists, as they shared both subjects and artistic concerns. Most painted directly from nature, recording impressions of Monhegan's constantly changing light and landscape. Occasionally, the style of one artist can be seen influencing another; Bogdanove's view of dories pulled up on Fish Beach, with its uncharacteristically pastel palette and swollen-bellied boats (pl. 37), pays direct homage to Hudson's work, both in style and subject. Bogdanove's own style was distinguished by its boldness, strength, and vigor. Lee Court(1903–1992), who joined Monhegan's community of artists in 1925, described Bogdanove as a "bombastic, explosive painter, and a good painter."[27] Thomas Ierardi, a painter who spent the summer of 1938 studying with Bogdanove, agreed, writing, "Bogdanove's paintings are rugged and forceful, just like Boggy who was five feet and three inches tall and 150 pounds of concentrated strength. The moods of his marines run from the emphatic and strong movement of surf and seas to the calm guarded light of foggy days."[28]

The island community also provided year-round support for its members. Theophile Schneider arranged for an exhibition of Bogdanove's marines in November 1930, at the Lamson and Hubbard Gallery in Boston, which attracted positive notice in the press. One reviewer observed:

> the canvases are well ballasted with rock, for they are of the bold headlands that barrier the northern coast against the predatory assaults of an angry sea. . . . Bogdanove is a serious painter, and his hard, crisp strokes of pigment applied impasto show his determination to realize the solidity of stone.[29]

From the time of his first solo exhibition in 1920, Bogdanove had worked aggressively in the winters to show his Maine paintings. His work was included in annual exhibitions at the National Academy of Design, the Pennsylvania Academy of the Fine Arts, the Carnegie Institute, and the Corcoran Gallery. By the late 1920s, he was represented by the Leonard Clayton Gallery in New York, which provided a regular venue for showing his new paintings. With this achievement came final and full recognition of Bogdanove's gifts as a marine painter. Comment on his work during the 1920s frequently presented him as a muralist foraying into new terrain, but by the 1930s his marines were accepted without qualification. As one reviewer enthused:

> With a wide brush and obvious love for the scene, A. J. Bogdanove paints rocks and the sea beating against them. Each picture varies with the varying light of the time of day. There is something lonely about these paintings and something inviting.[30]

Over time, Bogdanove came to be one of the artists who introduced Monhegan to a new generation of painters, just as Henri, Kent, Bellows, and Waugh had before him. Ted Davis (b. 1908) credited paintings by Bogdanove and Winter with attracting him to the island. As he recalled: "I had first come across Monhegan when I saw Andrew Winter's painting. . . . And the other one was an Abe Bogdanove . . . hanging on the wall of a gallery in New York. . . . It had the rugged coast that now I understand was Lobster Cove."[31]

Secure in his success, Bogdanove ventured further afield in search of new locales in the mid-1930s. Early in the summer of 1935, he traveled with his wife and two young sons to Canada's Gaspé Peninsula. There he made oil sketches of the cliffs and fishing villages which he brought back to be developed into paintings during the summer on Monhegan. Three years later, he took a semester's leave from teaching to travel with his family throughout Europe. It was the artist's second trip to the continent, and he visited Italy, Spain, France, Holland, and Great Britain. Once again, he found inspiration in coastal scenery, sketching in seaside villages in Italy, France, and England. The trip was marred by intimations of war—Hitler's rise prompted the family to cancel planned visits to Austria and Germany, and Bogdanove's application for a visa to Russia, his homeland, was denied without explanation. The artist and his family returned to Monhegan at the start of the summer, with a fresh appreciation of the island's tranquillity after the stress and turmoil of Europe.

Following his retirement from teaching at the College of the City of New York in 1942, Bogdanove made New England his year-round home. He moved with his family to

Dunbarton, New Hampshire, not far from Manchester. He settled there with the encouragement of Maude Briggs Knowlton (1870–1956), another Monhegan painter and the director of the Currier Gallery, who had "always been interested in him as a painter."[32] His snowy view of Manchester's Amoskeag Mills (pl. 34) records this new episode in his life. It was a tragically brief period, for the artist died suddenly and unexpectedly in 1946.

Bogdanove left a twofold legacy. His murals reflect the education and opportunities for artists coming of age at the turn of the century. Further, they record a moment when art was widely believed to contribute to the public good. Where his murals reflect his skills as an academic painter, Bogdanove's Maine paintings are the true expression of his creative identity. Bold and forceful, they are an evocation of their creator and speak to the special inspiration that Monhegan island offered, and continues to offer, artists. They recognize the foundations of that tradition in their allusions to the work of Homer, Henri, Kent, Bellows, and Hopper, and they extend Monhegan's rich art history into an era when a new community of artists developed a lasting bond with that place. Most importantly, they preserve the artistic journey of Abraham Bogdanove with a freshness and immediacy that makes them truly timeless.

Notes

1. While Bogdanove's *Self-portrait* is undated, a study of photographs of the artist suggest that it may be dated ca. 1935–1942. The seascape in the background is consistent with the palette used by the artist in his marines of that period. This *Self-portrait* is probably the work exhibited by Bogdanove in 1942 at the National Academy of Design's annual exhibition (April 8 –May 16).

2. Bogdanove received the second Hallgarten Prize in 1909 and the first in 1910 and 1911; he was also awarded the Cannon Prize for the best painting from the nude in 1909 and a first prize for figurative sculpture in 1910. Information courtesy of the National Academy of Design Archives. For the history of the Hallgarten Prize see, Eliot Clark, *History of the National Academy of Design* (New York: Columbia University Press, 1954), p. 136.

3. Helen Appleton Read, "Art," *The Brooklyn Daily Eagle,* January 21, 1918, p. 8; Bogdanove also worked as a studio assistant for the muralist Charles Yardley Turner. See Emmie B. Whitney, "Bogdanove, Painter of Marines and Murals, Finds Inspiration on Monhegan," *Lewiston Journal Illustrated Magazine* (September 14, 1935): 6A.

4. Emmie B. Whitney, "Bogdanove, Artist at Monhegan, Sees Decline of Art in Europe," *Lewiston Journal Magazine* (August 27, 1938), p. 7A.

5. "French, Russian, and American Paintings: Art at Home and Abroad," *New York Times Magazine,* April 7, 1918, p. 14.

6. "Mural Dedicated at Manual Training as War Memorial," *Brooklyn Daily Eagle,* November 9, 1922.

7. Of the murals executed by Bogdanove between 1918 and 1925 for Brooklyn's Commercial High School (now Paul Robeson High School), *Education* is still there; two others, *Ancient Commerce* and *Modern Commerce* were removed in 1992, conserved, and reinstalled at Tottenville High School, Staten Island; two paintings, *The Arrival of the Mayflower* (1926) and *The Caravels of Columbus* (1930), continue to hang in P.S. 43 in the Bronx; *Peace* survives, but has been removed from its original location; *The Great Teachers* (1930) is in its original location in Shepherd Hall at City College of The City University of New York.

8. Bogdanove exhibited *The Brook* at the National Academy of Design annual exhibition, March 18–April 23, 1916. This was the first of twelve works by the artist accepted for exhibition at the academy between 1916 and 1944. See, Peter Hastings Falk, ed., *The Annual Exhibition Record of the National Academy of Design 1910–1950* (Madison, Conn: Sound View Press, 1990), p. 87.

9. *Exhibition of Paintings by A. J. Bogdanove* (New York: Young Men's Hebrew Association, 1920). The show was held from April 17 to May 22, 1920.

10. Whitney 1935, p. 6A.

11. Robert Henri to Richard and Theresa Lee, July 12, 1903, Henri Papers, The Yale Collection of American Literature, Beinecke Rare Book and Manuscript Library, Yale University, New Haven, Connecticut.

12. Bruce St. John, ed., *John Sloan's New York Scene* (New York: Harper & Row, 1965), p. 121.

13. Bogdanove was part of a group of artists exhibiting at The MacDowell Club in New York City in October 1918.

14. Falk 1990, pp. 530–531.

15. Robert Henri, *The Art Spirit* (Philadelphia: J.B. Lippincott Company, 1923), p. 118.

16. Leon Kroll, *A Spoken Memoir,* Nancy Hale and Fredson Bowers, eds. (Charlottesville, Va.: University Press of Virginia, 1983), p. 14.

17. "Paintings A. J. Bogdanove," exh. announcement (New York: The Incurable Collector, 1965).

18. Henri to Frank Southern, September 7, 1918, Henri Papers.

19. "Maker of Poster Smash the Hun is Visitor Here," *Portland Evening Express and Daily Advertiser,* August 23, 1918, p. 20.

20. Whitney 1935, p. 7A.

21. Rockwell Kent, *It's Me O Lord* (New York: Dodd, Mead & Company, 1955), p. 131.

22. Ruth Grant Faller, *Monhegan: Her Houses and Her People, 1780–1970* (Melrose, Mass.: Mainstay Publications, 1995), p. 55.

23. Whitney 1935, p. 6A.

24. Whitney 1935, p. 6A.

25. Dr. Maximilian Toch, "Introduction," in *Recent Marine Paintings of the Coast of Maine by A. J. Bogdanove* (New York: Leonard Clayton Gallery, 1936). Toch and Bogdanove had worked together to develop binders that would eliminate fading in oil paintings.

26. Interview with Julie and Jackie Hudson by Ed Deci, July 30, 1990. Transcript in the collection of the Monhegan Museum, Maine.

27. Interview with Lee W. Court by Ed Deci, Summer 1990, Monhegan Museum.

28. Reminiscence of Dr. Thomas Ierardi, August 6, 1980, Archives, Spanierman Gallery, LLC, New York.

29. "Canvases Well Ballasted," newspaper clipping dated November 12, 1930, in, *Cabot Album,* vol. III, part II, Monhegan Library, Maine.

30. "Comment on the Week's Exhibitions," *New York Times,* October 27, 1929, unpaged Bogdanove clipping file, New York Public Library.

31. Interview with Ted Davis by Ed Deci, July 30, 1990, Monhegan Museum.

32. Interview with Jackie Hudson by Jessica Nicoll, July 30, 1996, Monhegan, Maine.

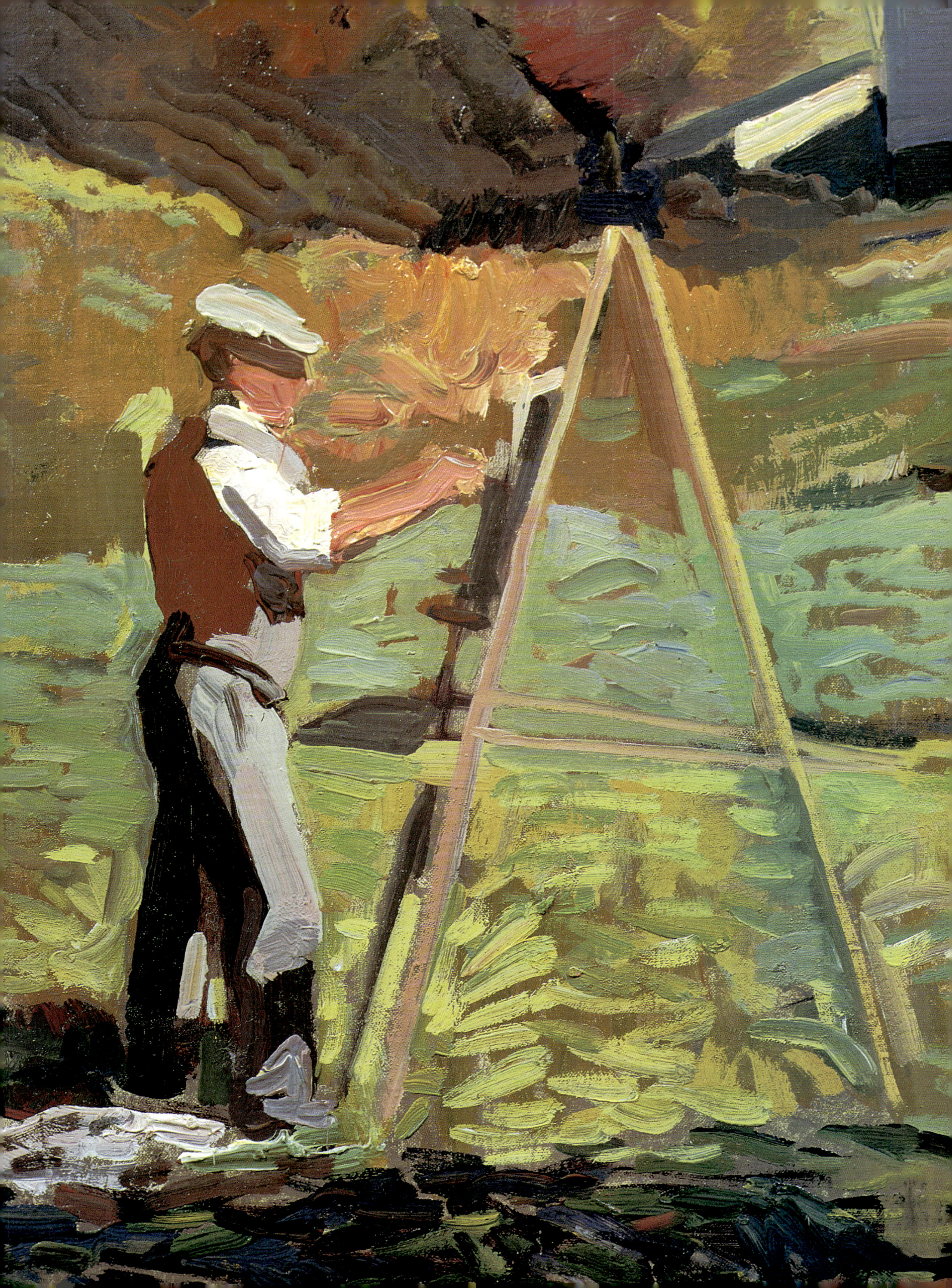

1.

Little White Head, ca. 1920–1935

Oil on canvas

25 × 30 in. (63.5 × 76.2 cm)

Signed lower center: *A. J. Bogdanove*

Little White Head was a favorite subject for Bogdanove—he exhibited a painting titled *Little White Head* at the Young Men's Hebrew Association in 1920 and again at the Lamson & Hubbard Gallery in Boston in 1930. Like Bogdanove's other depiction of Little White Head in this catalogue (pl. 19), this work was painted at the water's edge, a position that dramatizes the scale of the rocks. However, the tide is higher in this view than in the other image, and therefore, the coastal formation is counterbalanced by an active sea.

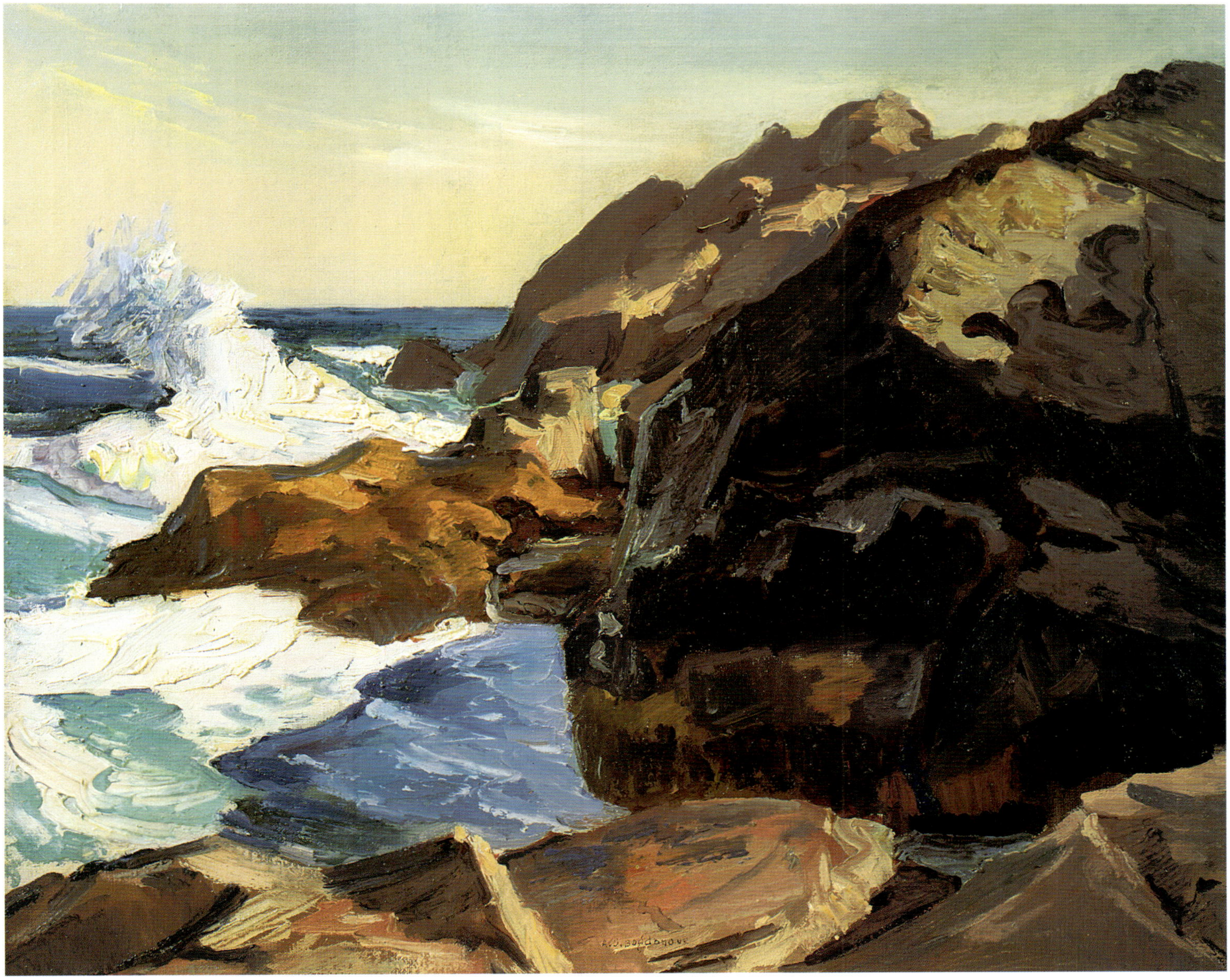

2.

Large Boat and Small, ca. 1935–1938

Oil on canvasboard
19⅞ × 24 in. (50.4 × 61 cm)
Signed lower right: *A. J. Bogdanove*
Inscribed on verso: *Large Boat and Small*

Large Boat and Small offers a view of Monhegan's harbor in brilliant sunlight. With a drydocked boat seen prominently in the foreground on an open stretch of beach and only a single smaller vessel visible on the water, the painting conveys the quietude of the island's shore. The land mass in the background is Manana Island, which, lying to the west of Monhegan, offers shelter to the larger island's harbor. The light palette used in this work is characteristic of Bogdanove's paintings of the mid-1930s.

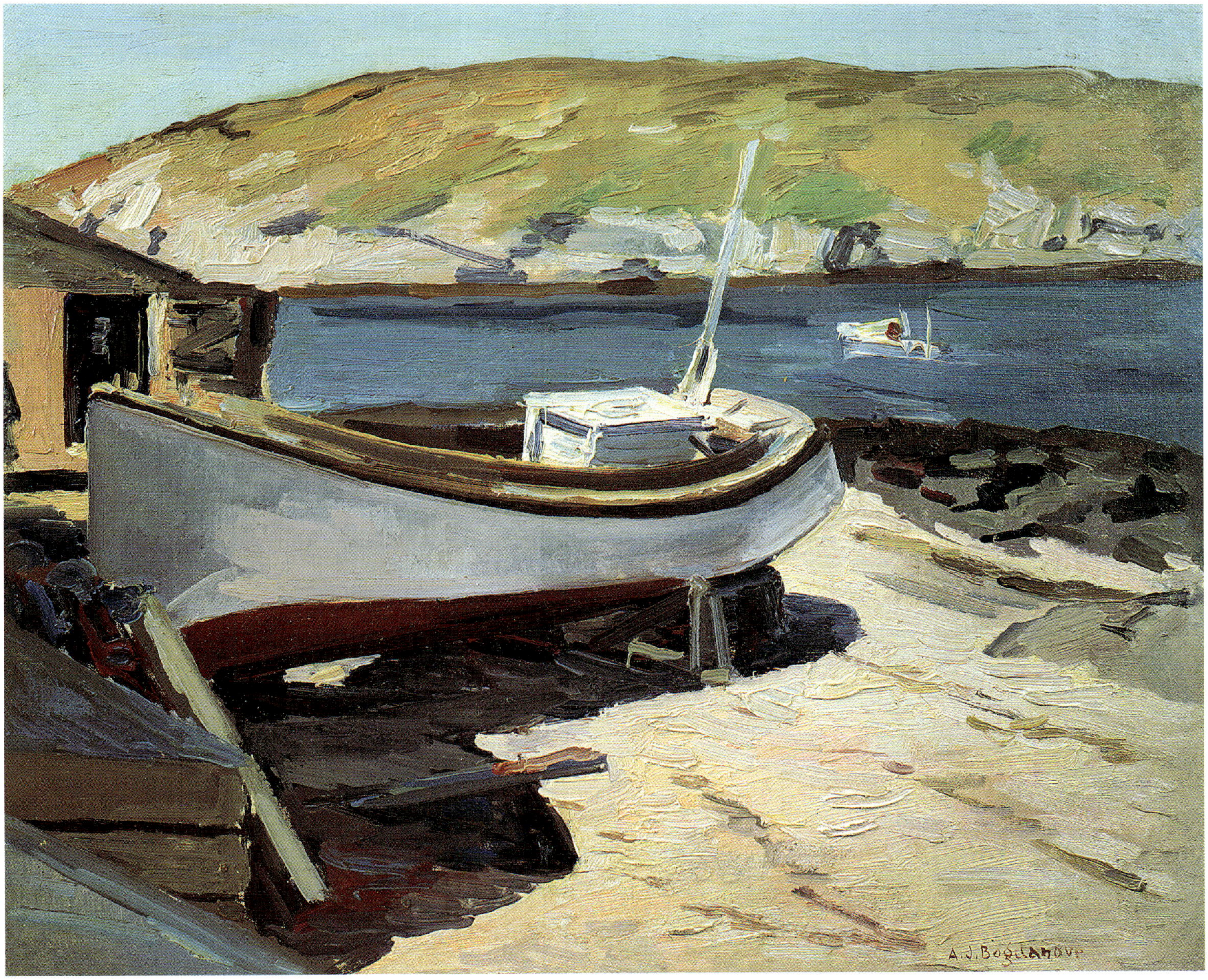
A.J. Bogdanove

3.

Low Tide Surf, ca. 1940

Oil on masonite
30 × 36 in. (76.2 × 91.4 cm)
Signed lower right: *A. J. Bogdanove*

Low Tide Surf demonstrates Bogdanove's masterful ability to convey the power of the Atlantic Ocean. Positioning the viewer in the scene's jagged rocky foreground, Bogdanove compels us to confront the oncoming surf. The low vantage point and the focus on one crashing wave intensify the scene's impact. Bogdanove's closely cropped and minimalist composition is reminiscent of the stark and simplified designs in Winslow Homer's views of the sea crashing against rocks in Prout's Neck, Maine, that were rendered at the turn of the twentieth century.

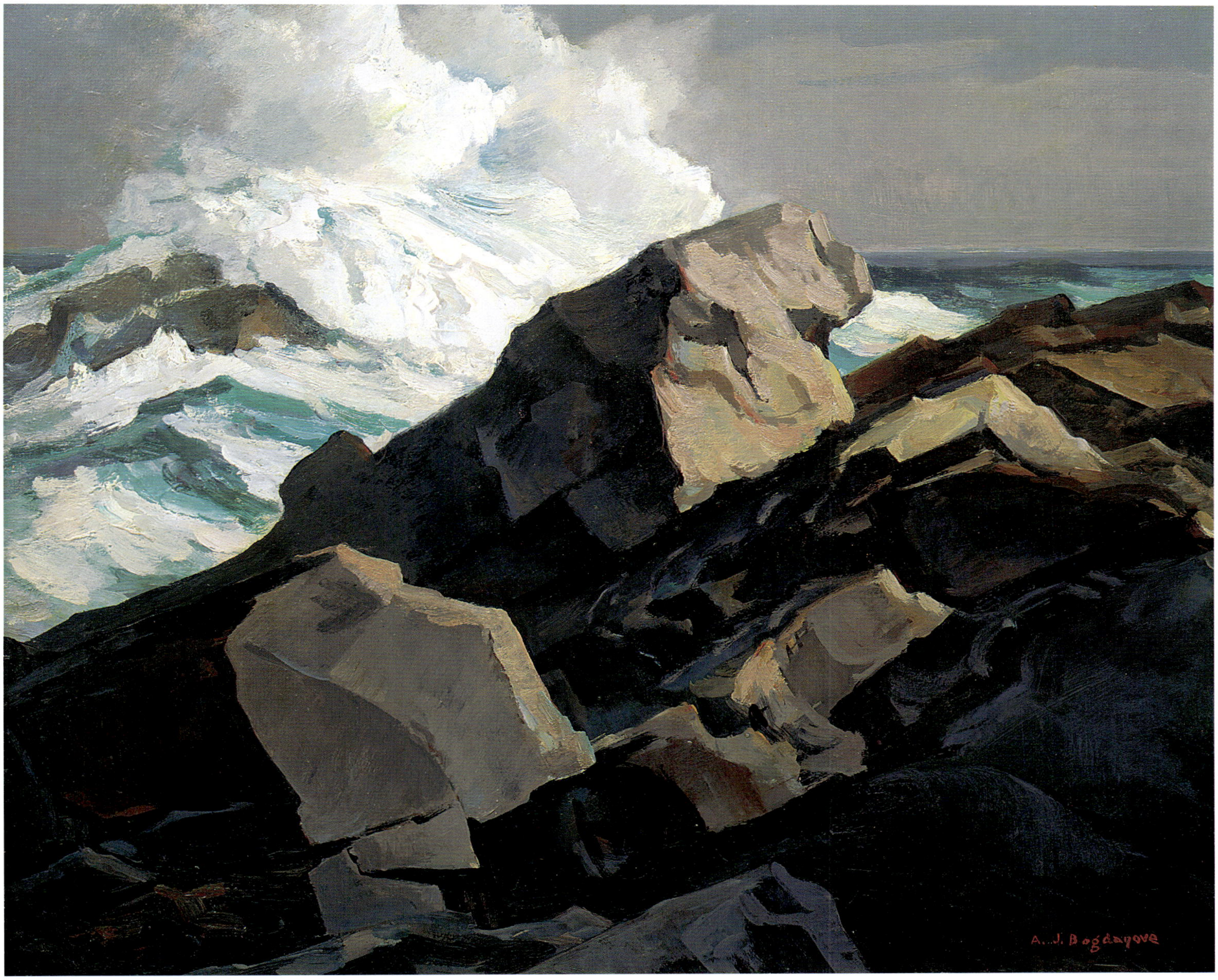
A. J. Bogdanove

4.

Fisherman's Shack, ca. 1930–1940

Oil on canvas
20 × 30 in. (50.8 × 76.2 cm)
Signed lower right: *A. J. Bogdanove*

Fisherman's Shack is more literally realistic than many of Bogdanove's renderings of Monhegan's houses. The careful delineation of the building's geometry emphasizes that this is a composition based almost entirely on diagonals and verticals. This focus on compositional structure recalls George Bellows's late work, while the painting's linearity, the flatness of the sky, and the way that light defines the planes of building walls is reminiscent of Edward Hopper's many similar scenes.

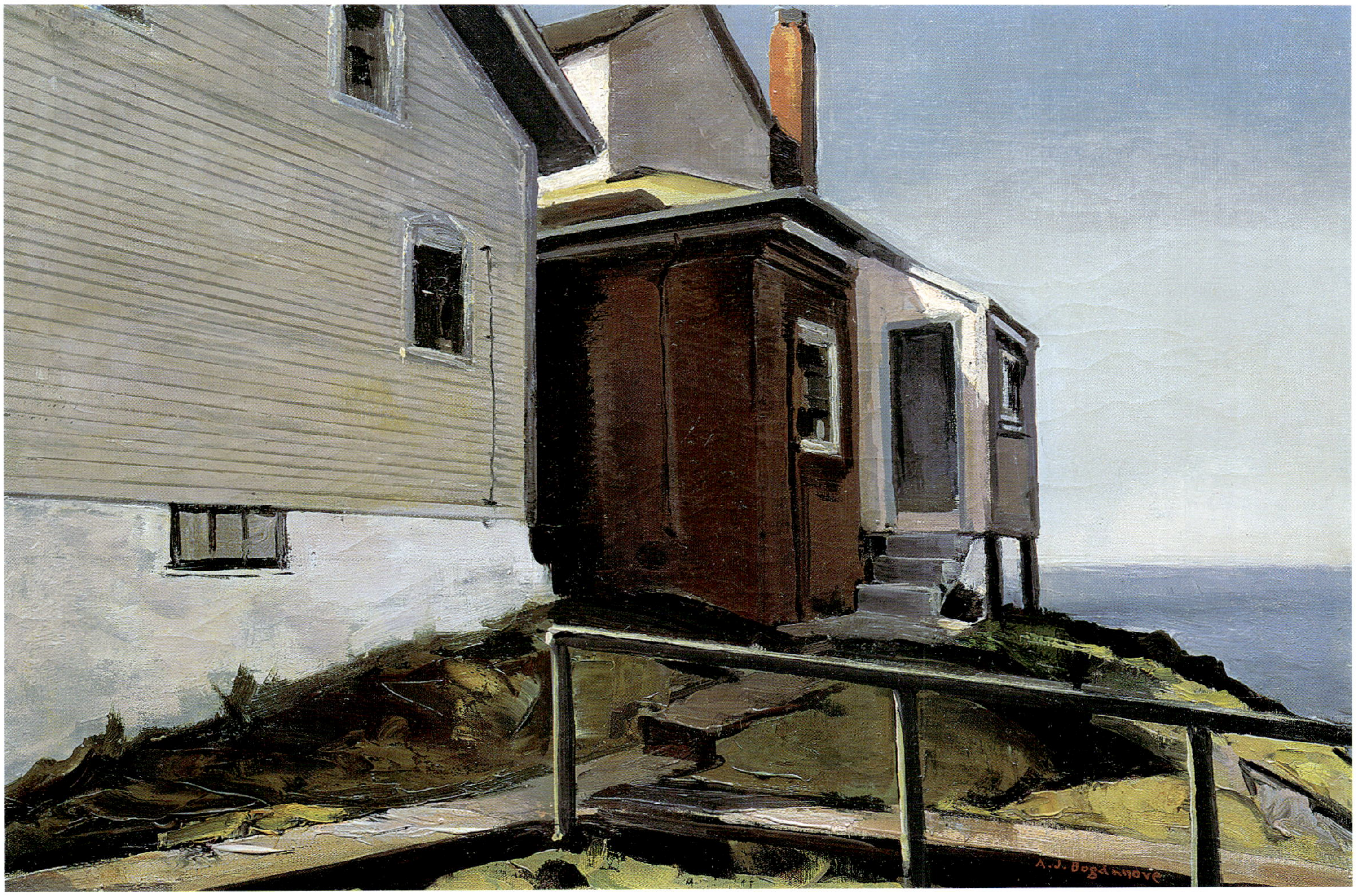
A. J. Bogdanove

5.

Summer Landscape, ca. 1912–1917

Oil on canvas
16 × 20 in. (40.6 × 50.8 cm)
Signed lower right: *A. J. Bogdanove*

Summer Landscape features the pastel palette and Impressionist brushwork typical of Bogdanove's early landscapes. It may have been painted in the countryside outside of New York City or on Maine's Mount Desert Island which the artist visited during the summers of 1915 through 1917. Its raised vantage point is distinctive, offering a more panoramic view than many of his later paintings.

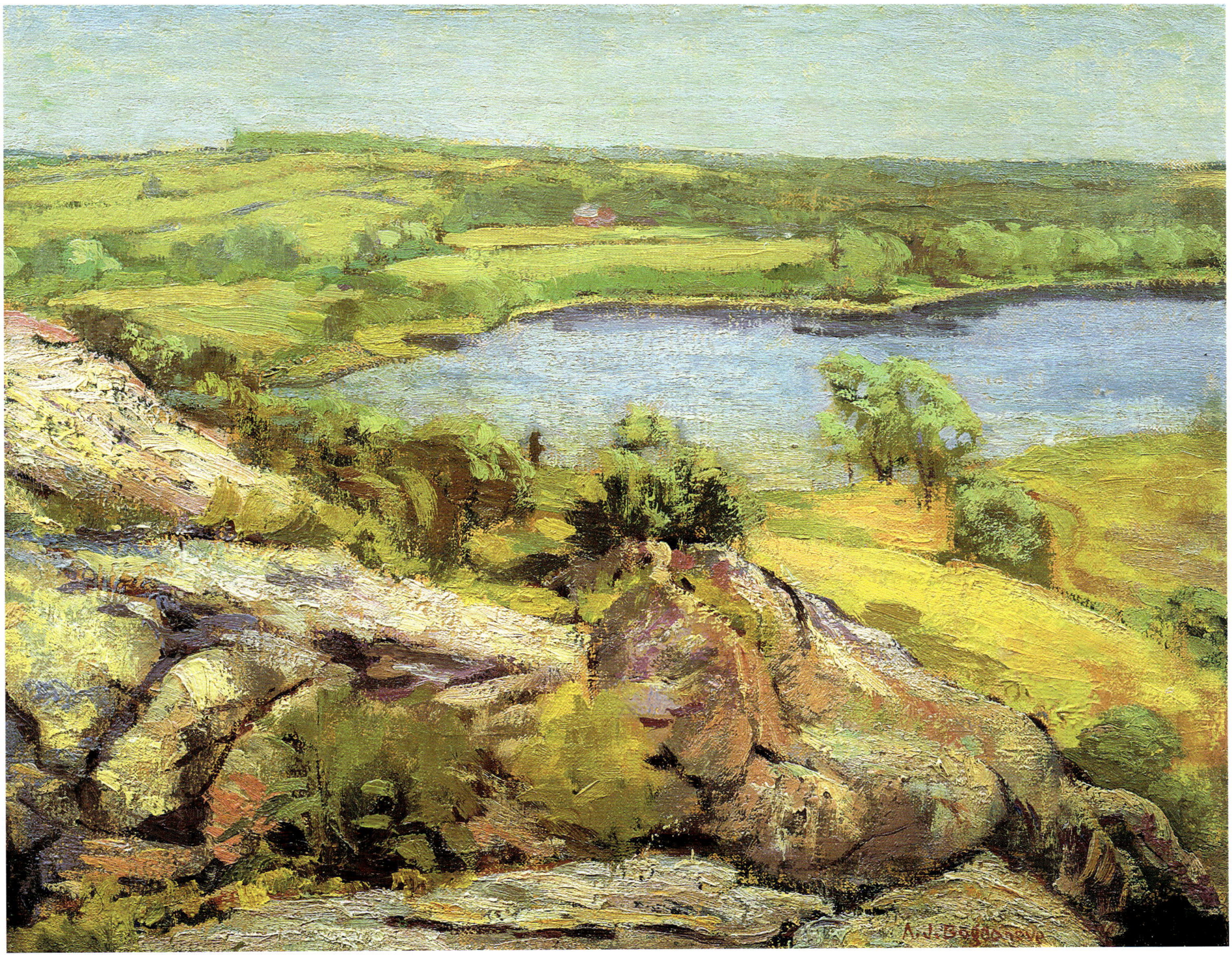

6.

The Harbor, ca. 1925–1935

Oil on canvasboard
12 × 16 in. (30.5 × 40.6 cm)
Signed lower left: *A. J. Bogdanove*
Inscribed on verso: *The Harbor*

The focal point of this painting is the coast guard boathouse on the shore of Manana Island, which stood until 1992, when it was washed away by a storm. The ladder-like structure descending the hill at the left is a tramway used to transport supplies to the fog signal station on the other side of Manana. Portraying the boathouse from the village of Monhegan, directly across the harbor, Bogdanove accentuated the contrast between the modest white structure and the steeply ascending rocky cliff behind it, which the artist painted in deep, rich tones. A label on the reverse side of *The Harbor* indicates that it was shown in a summer exhibition at New York's Salmagundi Club, which Bogdanove joined in 1934.

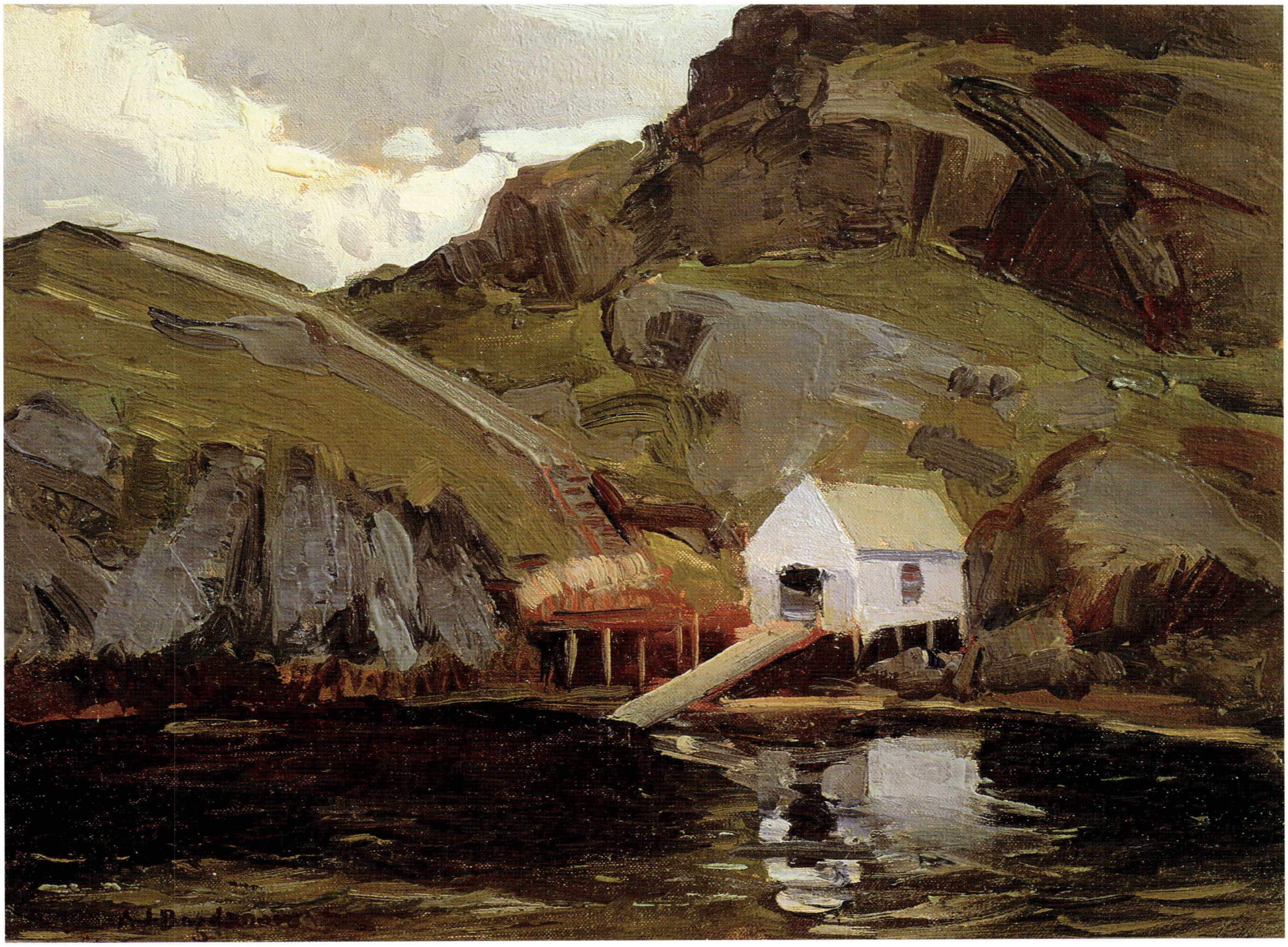

7.

Black Head, 1929

Oil on canvas
24⅞ × 30 in. (63.1 × 76.2 cm)
Signed and dated lower left: *A. J. Bogdanove 1929*
Inscribed on verso: *Black Head*

Among Monhegan's most breathtaking geological features are the headlands that tower above the open ocean, including Black Head, White Head, and Burnt Head. Bogdanove's view of Black Head captures its distinctive profile and soaring height. Rather than presenting the cliff as a static mass, the artist brought out the multicolored shadows and reflections on its craggy surface, investing the rock faces with a dynamism that contrasts with the comparatively calm sea below.

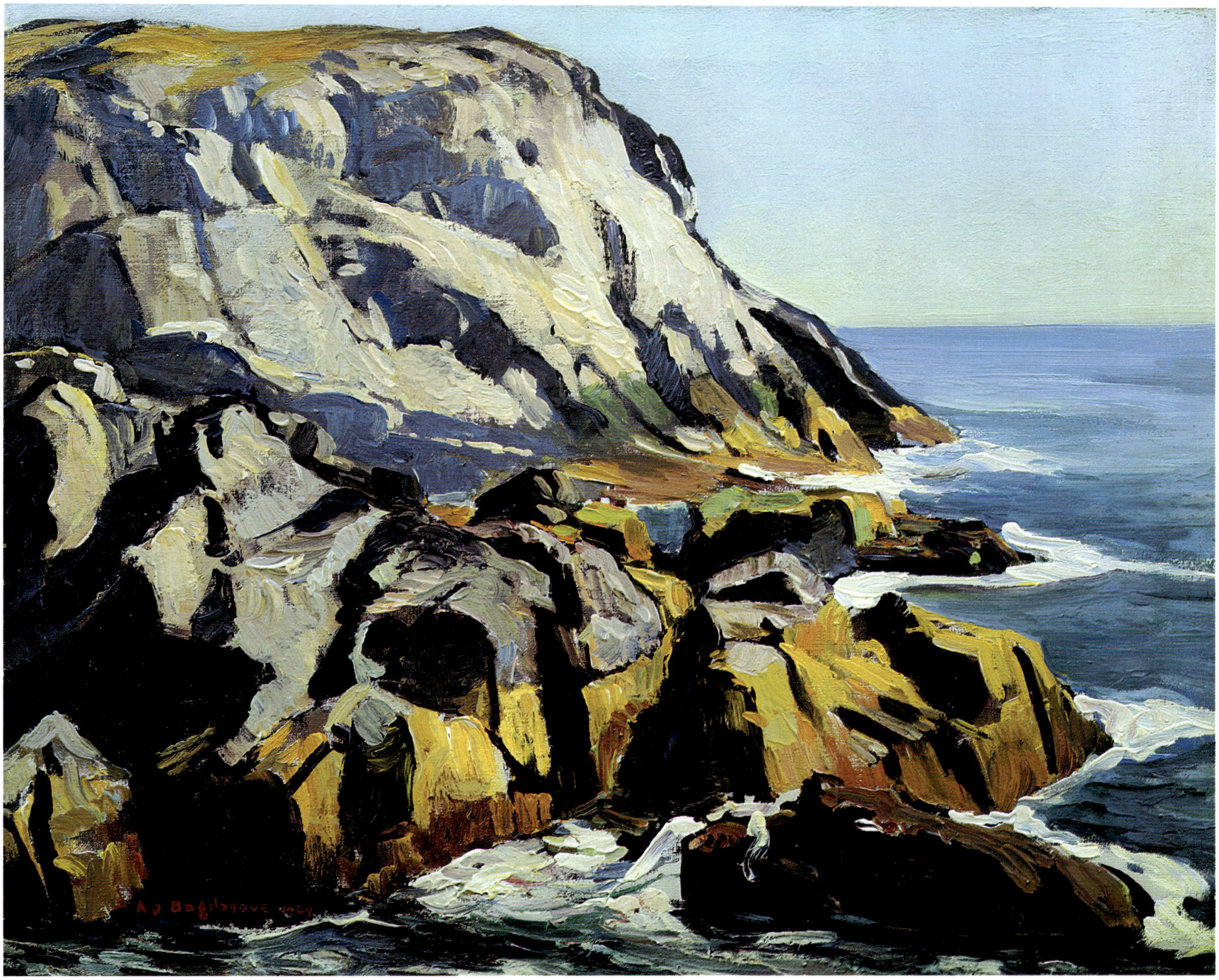

8.

Drydock, ca. 1935–1945

Oil on canvas
20 × 24 in. (50.8 × 61 cm)
Signed lower right: *A. J. Bogdanove*

Drydock underscores Bogdanove's fascination with the way a scene is altered by changing light or weather. The painting portrays virtually the same subject as *Boat and Boathouse* (pl. 33), however in that painting, Manana is completely obscured by a veil of fog. In *Drydock,* by contrast, Bogdanove captured the softening impact of diffused light on the scene. Lavender tones dominate in the architectural structure as well as in the landscape. The closely cropped composition focuses our attention on the graceful curve of the foreshortened boat in the foreground.

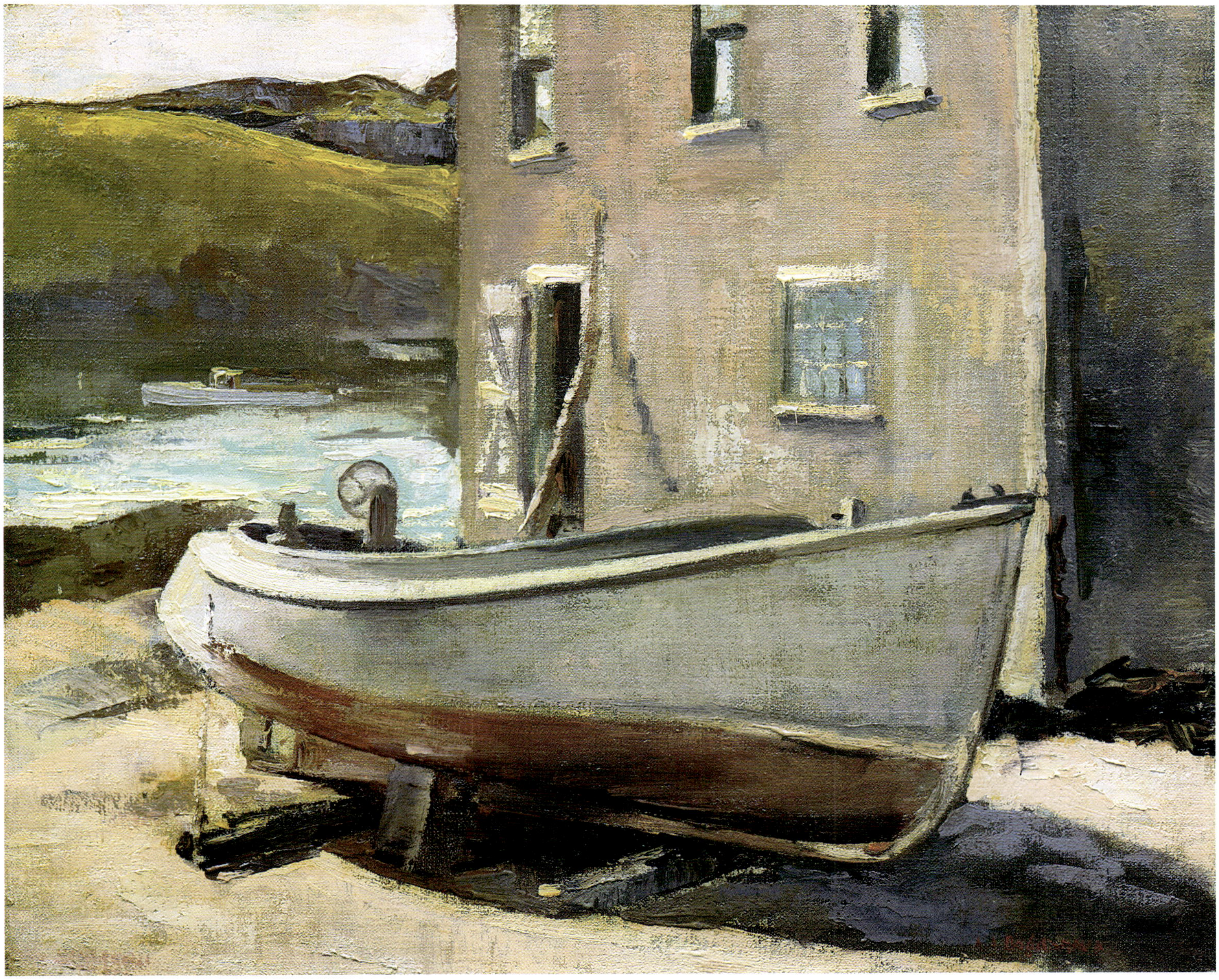

9.

The Pulpit, ca. 1930–1940

Oil on canvas

30 × 36 in. (76.2 × 91.4 cm)

Inscribed on verso: *The Pulpit*

Pulpit Rock is situated at the northern end of Monhegan Island, just beyond Black Head. Its name derives from its striking resemblance to a church pulpit when viewed from the ocean, and Bogdanove captured its unique and immediately recognizable shape in this painting. Indeed, the site was one that Bogdanove often enjoyed painting; he exhibited views of Pulpit Rock at the City Club of New York in 1925, at the National Academy of Design in 1928, and at the Lamson & Hubbard Gallery in Boston in 1930.

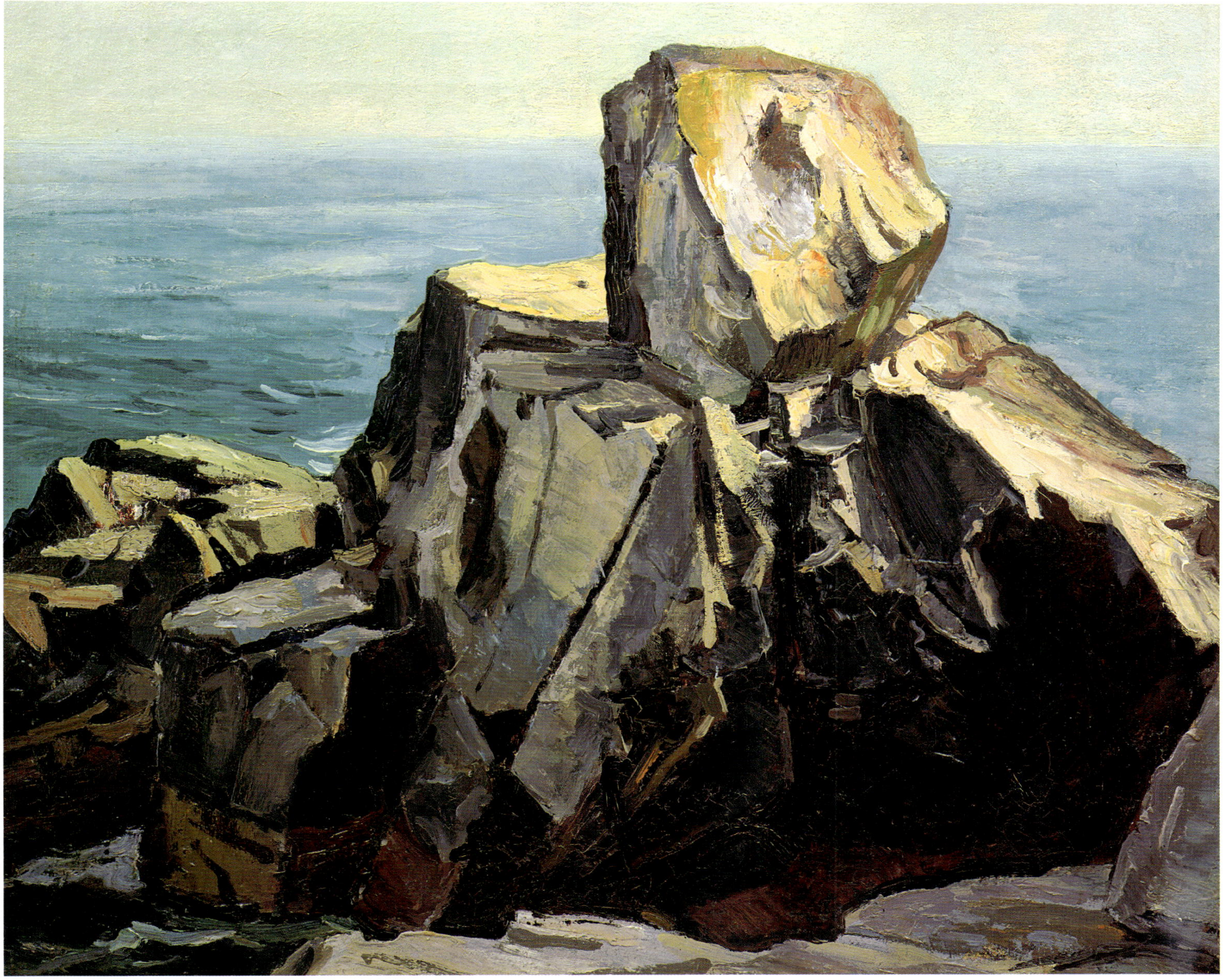

10.

Woman in Fur, ca. 1930–1940

Oil on canvas
40 × 36 in. (101.6 × 91.4 cm)

During the years that he was actively engaged as a muralist, Bogdanove was frequently occupied with important portrait commissions. While living in New York during the winters, he was often commissioned to do formal likenesses, in which he strictly adhered to the formulas for commemorative portraiture. In this painting, however, he departed from convention to produce a more casual image. The subject's informal pose and introspective gaze imbue the work with intimacy, which suggests that the sitter may have been a friend. The directness of the portrayal and the strong use of black are reminiscent of the bold portraits created by Robert Henri earlier in the century. Indeed, while presenting a vivid likeness, the painting can also be seen as an abstract study in blacks.

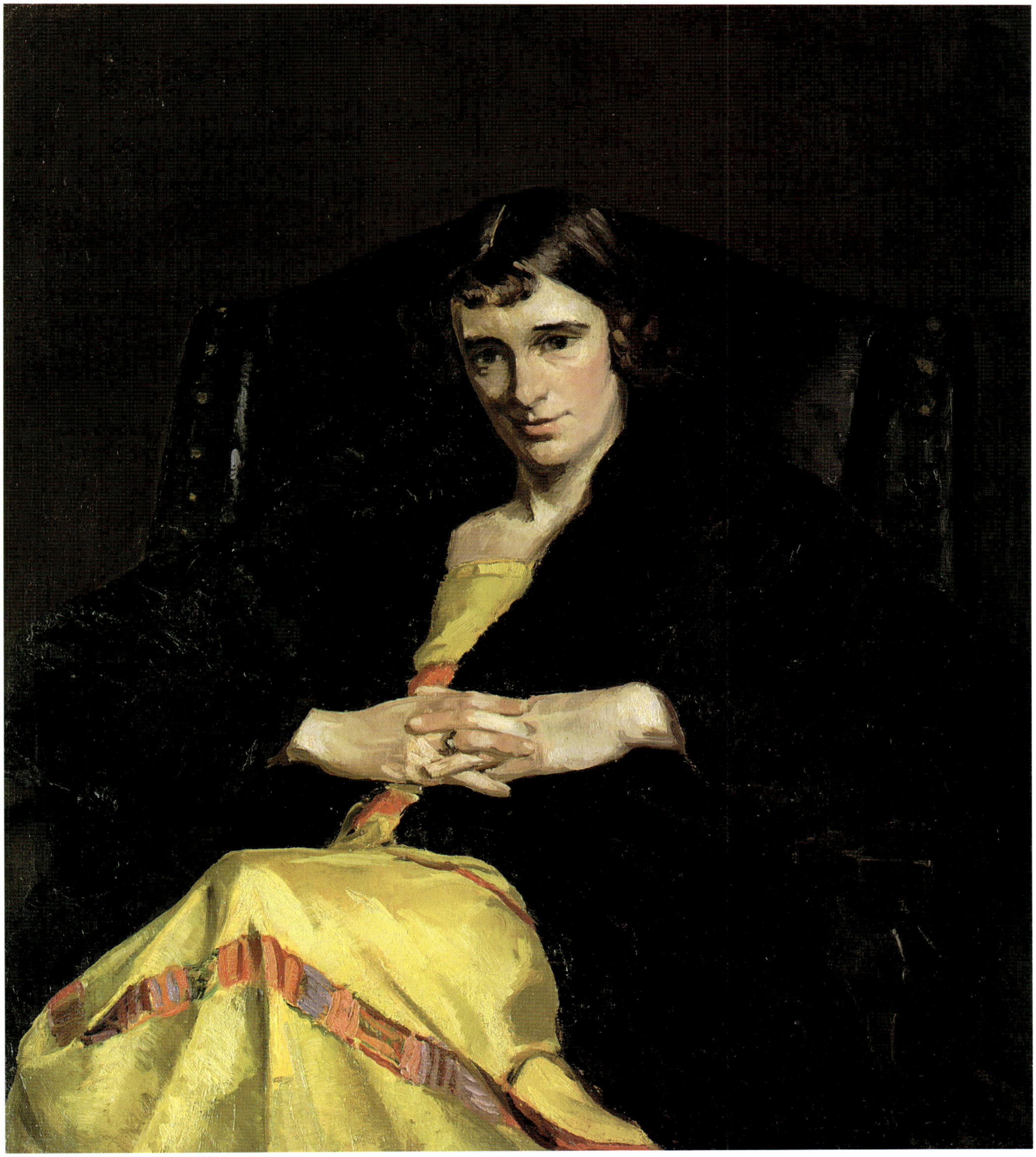

11.

Study for the Great Teachers Mural, 1928

Gouache on board

12⅛ × 40 in. (30.8 × 101.6 cm)

Signed, dated, and inscribed lower right: *© 1928 by A. J. Bogdanove / scale ¾″ = 1′ 0″*

Signed and inscribed on verso: *The Great Teachers. By A. J. Bogdanove / for Mural Painting for College of the City of New York*

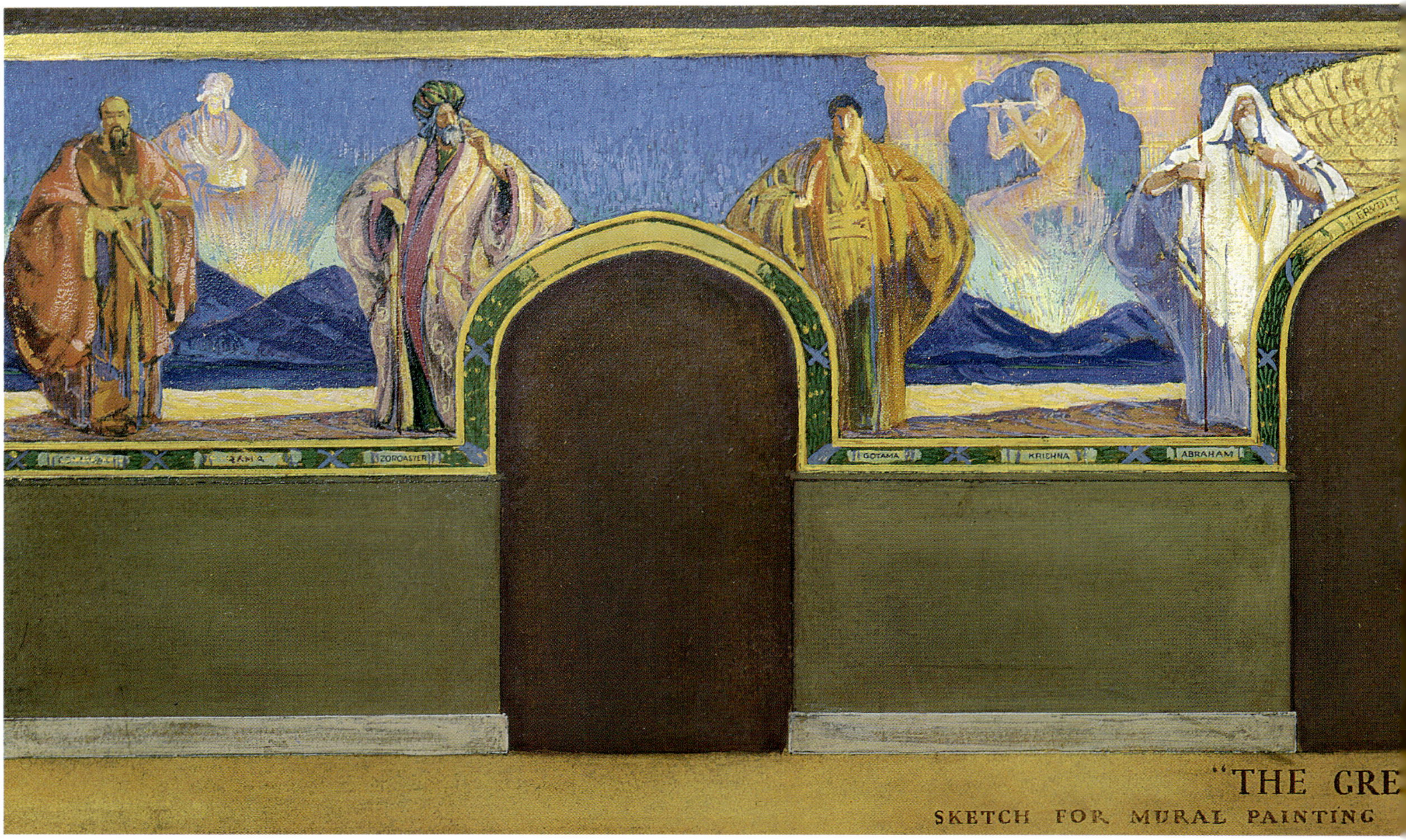

In the process of receiving approval for his mural designs for public buildings, Bogdanove created fully realized studies that demonstrated both a mural's imagery and its scale. One of these studies, created for Bogdanove's last mural, *The Great Teachers,* reveals his approach. Completed in 1930, this mural, which includes draped figures above arched portals, celebrates the legacy of great thinkers and teachers ranging from Confucius to Socrates. *The Great Teachers* still hangs in Shepherd Hall on the campus of City College of The City University of New York.

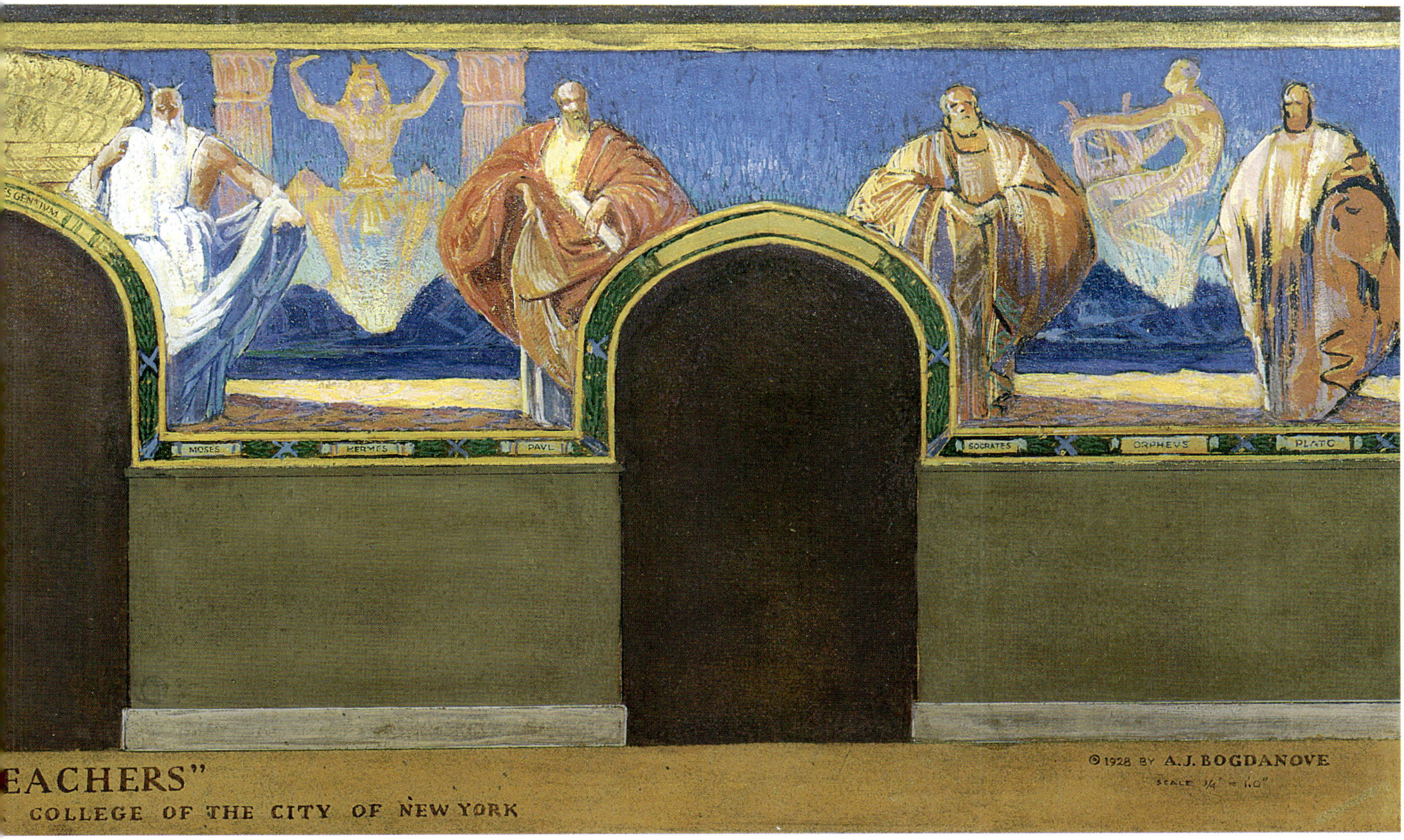
MOSES
HERMES
PAUL
SOCRATES
ORPHEUS
PLATO
EACHERS"
COLLEGE OF THE CITY OF NEW YORK
© 1928 BY A.J. BOGDANOVE

12.

Pearl, ca. 1935–1942

Oil on canvas

36 × 30 in. (91.4 × 76.2 cm)

Inscribed on verso: *Pearl*

Bogdanove may have painted *Pearl,* a portrait of his wife, about the same time as his *Self-portrait* (fig. 1). Both paintings show their subjects against the backdrop of crashing waves. However, whereas Bogdanove positioned himself in direct opposition to the sea, he portrayed his wife within the shelter of the rocks, as if to protect her from the ocean's swells.

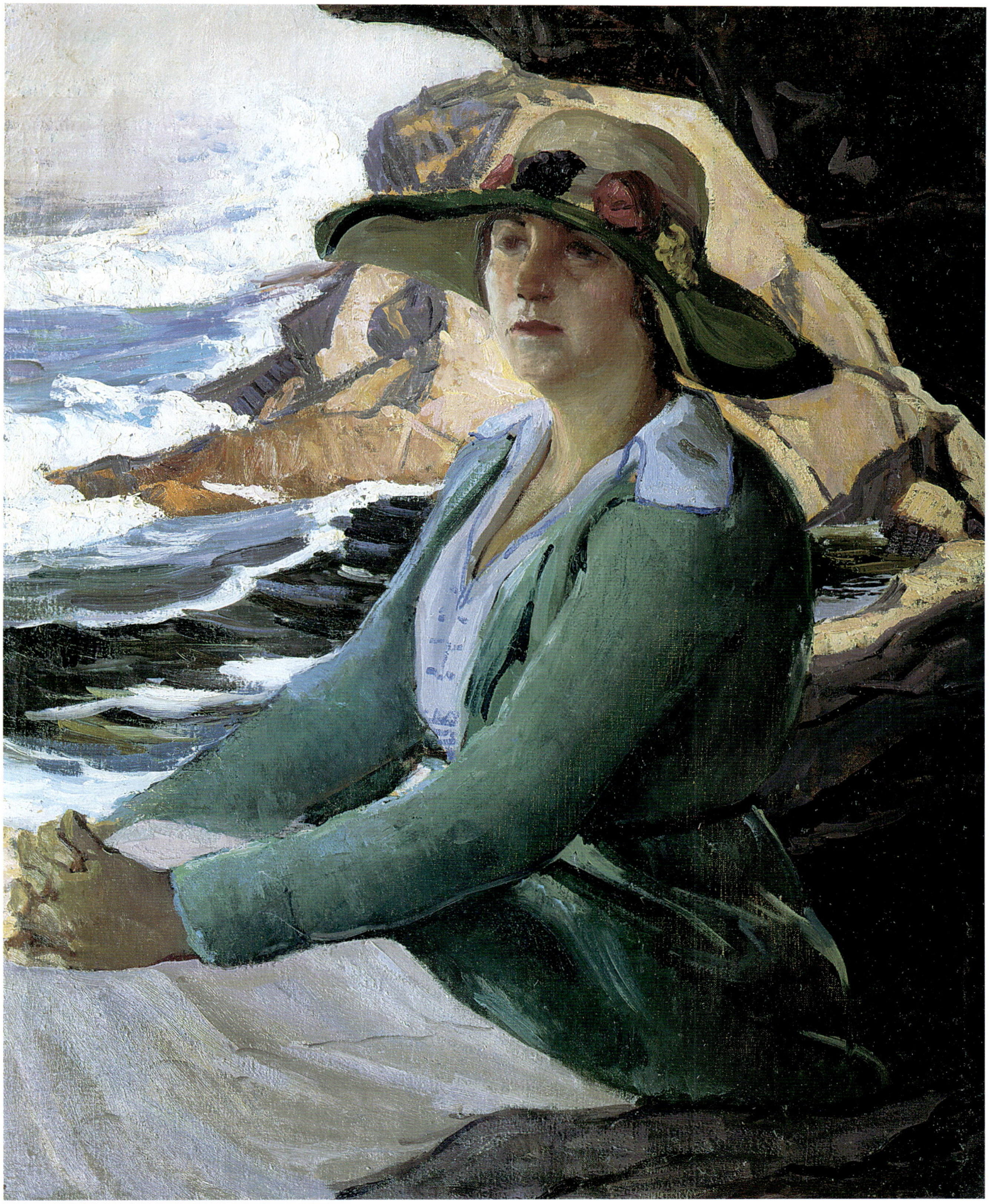

13.

Greenpoint, ca. 1925–1935

Oil on canvasboard
20 × 24 in. (50.8 × 61 cm)
Signed lower left and lower right: *A. J. Bogdanove*

Bogdanove rendered *Greenpoint* from this low spot at the northern end of Monhegan Island, which provides a view across the water toward Manana and Smutty Nose islands. The intense coloration of this painting recalls some of John Sloan's Gloucester paintings, particularly the salmon-pink tones of the rocks. The strong, abstract quality of the rocks in the foreground are typical of Bogdanove's work during this period.

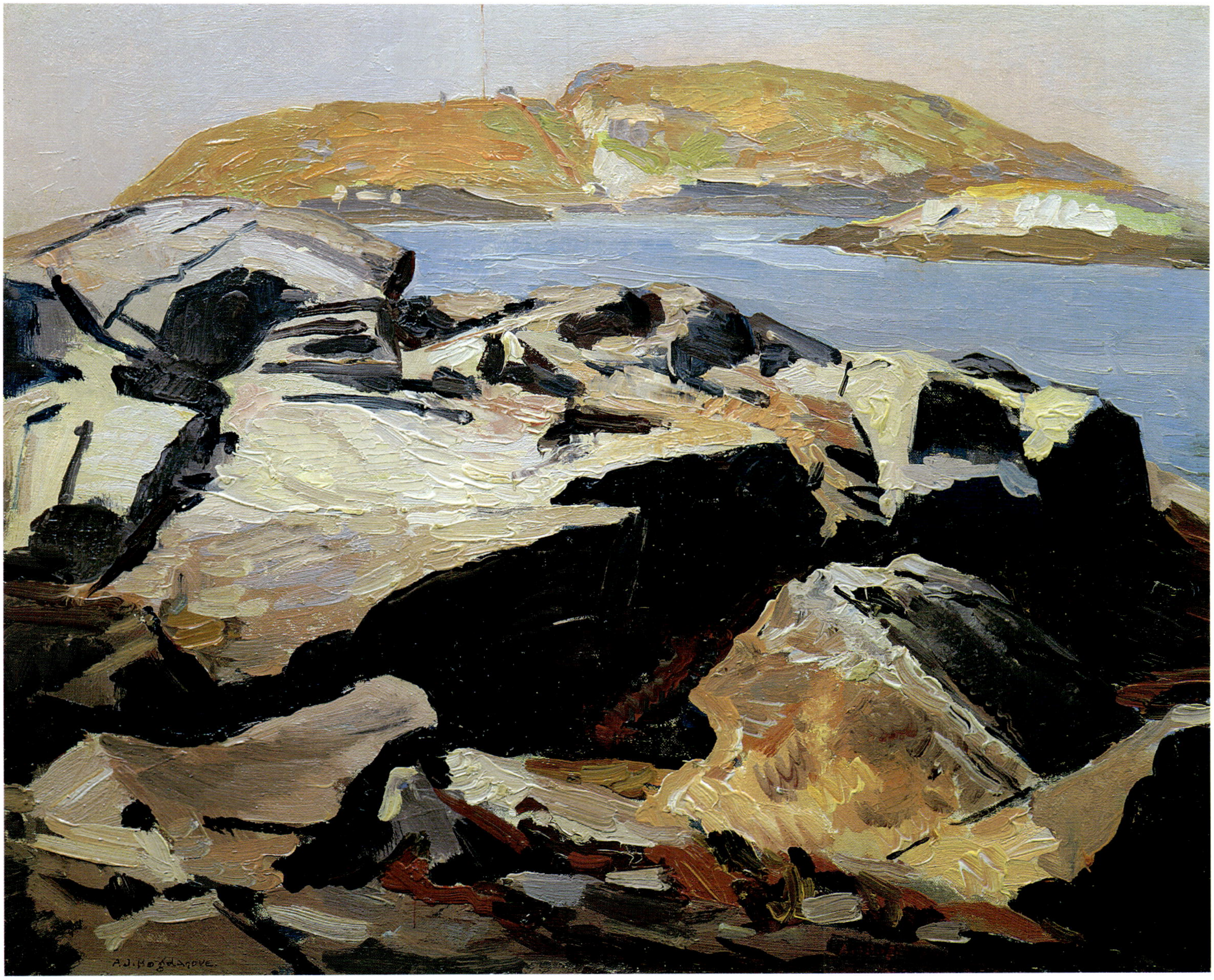

14.

Camerie Boats, France, 1938

Oil on board
13 × 16 in. (33 × 40.6 cm)
Inscribed on verso: *Camerie Boats*

In 1938, Bogdanove traveled to Europe, where he visited museums in Italy, Spain, France, Holland, and Great Britain and sketched in Normandy and on the Cornwall coast of England. To create his sketches, Bogdanove stocked up on thirteen-by-sixteen-inch panels in Paris, which were easily portable and afforded the possibility of plein-air painting. With his panels in hand, the artist sought out new painting sites, but he was attracted primarily to the same sort of coastal scenery that he had been depicting in America. In *Camerie Boats,* which he executed on one of the panels he purchased in Paris, he portrayed a scene possibly of the Brittany coastal town of Cameret, featuring beached boats silhouetted against a sandy shoreline. The boats could readily be Monhegan schooners, and the tranquility of the site is reminiscent of the New England coast.

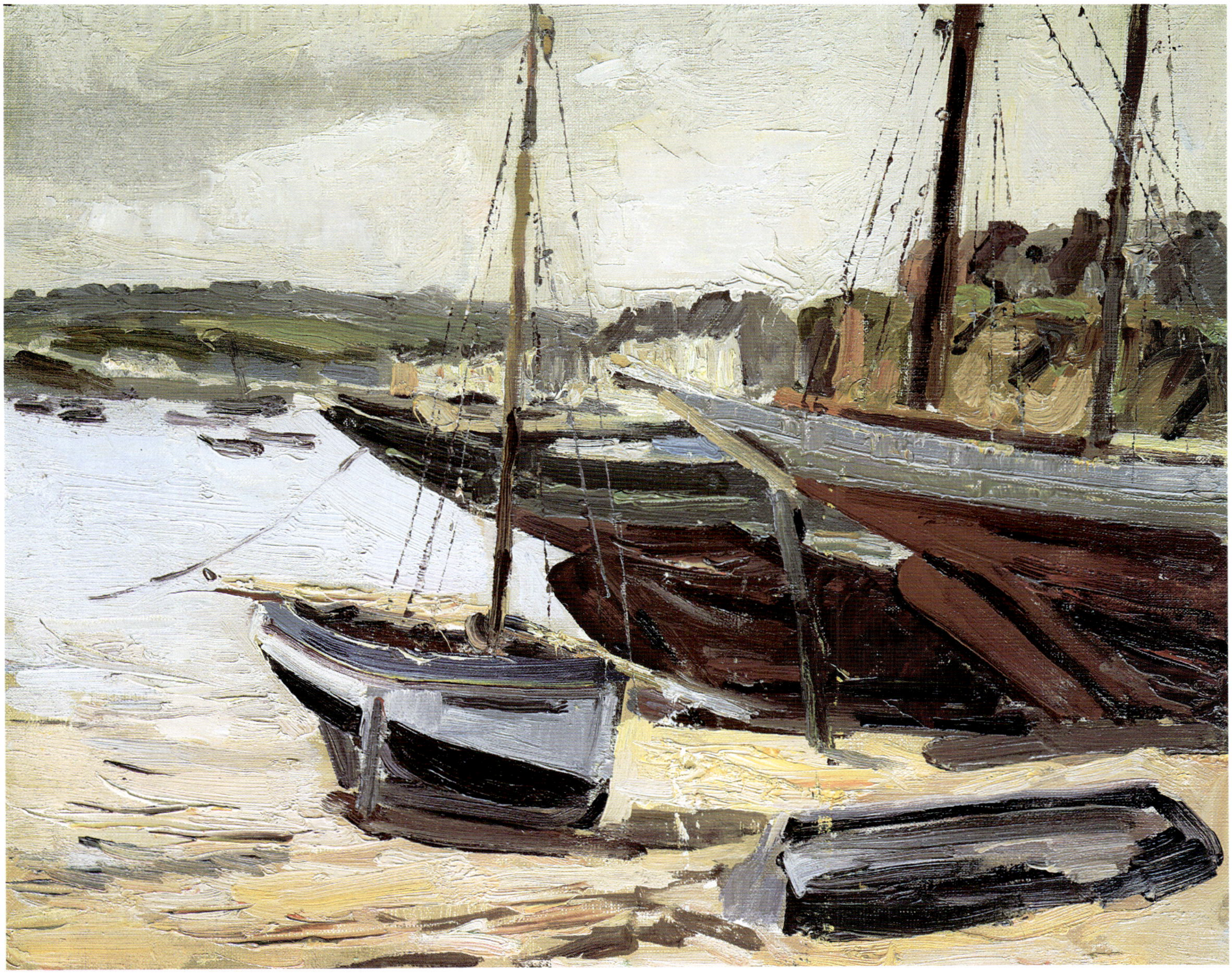

15.

Creek Woods, Connecticut, 1914

Oil on canvas

16 × 20 in. (40.6 × 50.8 cm)

Signed and dated lower left: *A. J. Bogdanove 1914*

Signed, dated, and inscribed on verso: *A. J. Bogdanove, 1914, Creek Woods, Connecticut*

Creek Woods, Connecticut is one of Bogdanove's earliest documented landscapes. It was painted in 1914, during a time when the artist was seeking to branch out from the mural painting work that had brought him success in New York City and was beginning to explore landscape painting. To study nature directly, Bogdanove traveled to the countrysides of New Jersey and Connecticut, where he painted outdoors and began to develop a more personalized style. Revealing Bogdanove's innate feeling for color and compositional balance, *Creek Woods, Connecticut* demonstrates the artist's confidence and skill during this period in his career.

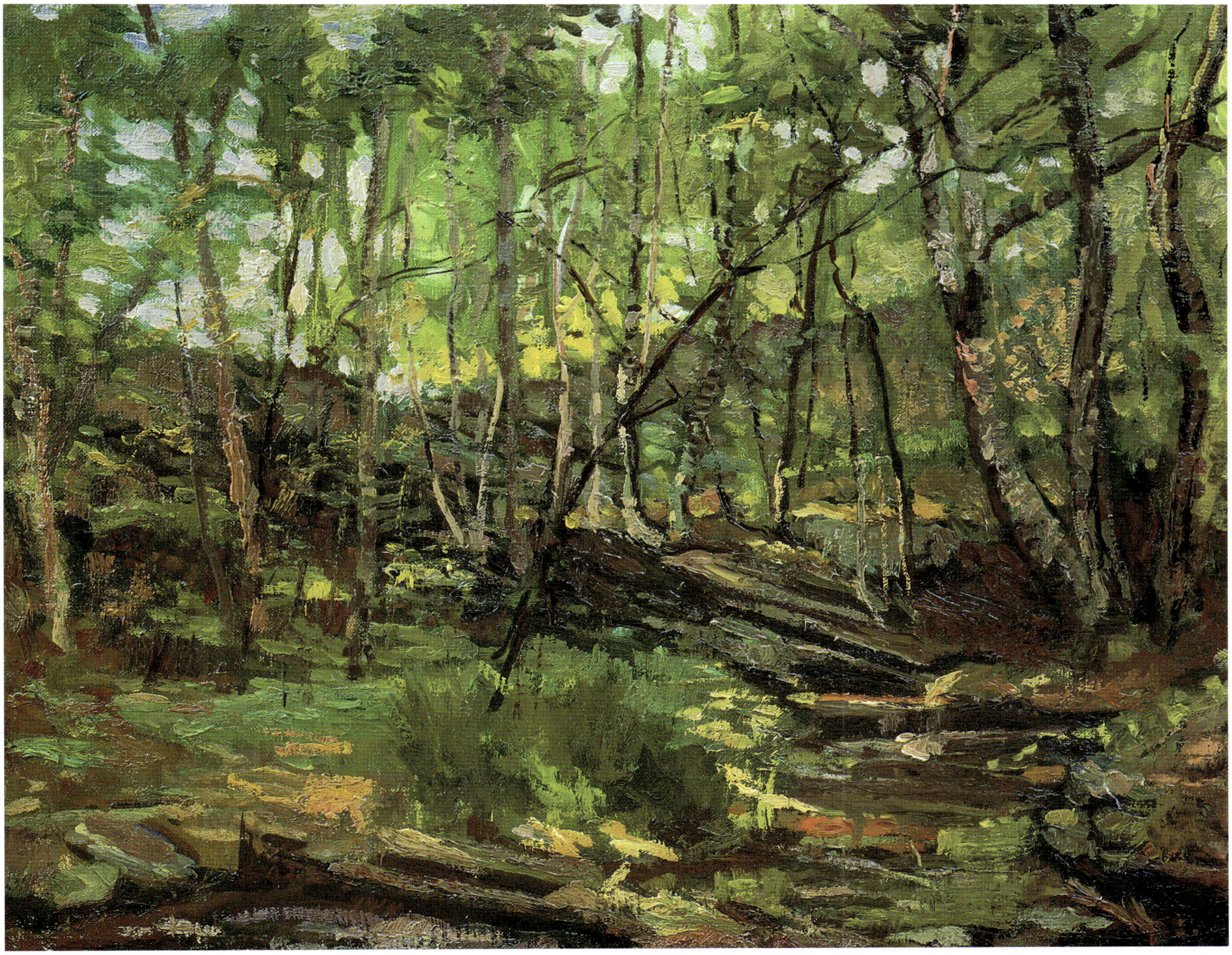

16.

Lobster Pots, ca. 1940–1945

Oil on board
8 × 10 in. (20.3 × 2.54 cm)
Inscribed on verso: *Lobster Pots*

Monhegan Island's season for lobster fishing is limited to the first six months of the year, and during the summer months, unused lobsters pots can be seen stacked picturesquely around most of the Island's houses. Taking advantage of the artistic possibilities of this subject, in *Lobster Pots,* Bogdanove created a composition that is both immediately recognizable and highly abstract. By broadly delineating the gables of lobster shacks, he focuses the viewer's attention on the pure geometry of the buildings. Incorporating the color and texture of the panel into the image, he used its warm-brown tone to define the edge of the road and the spaces between the slats of the lobster pots.

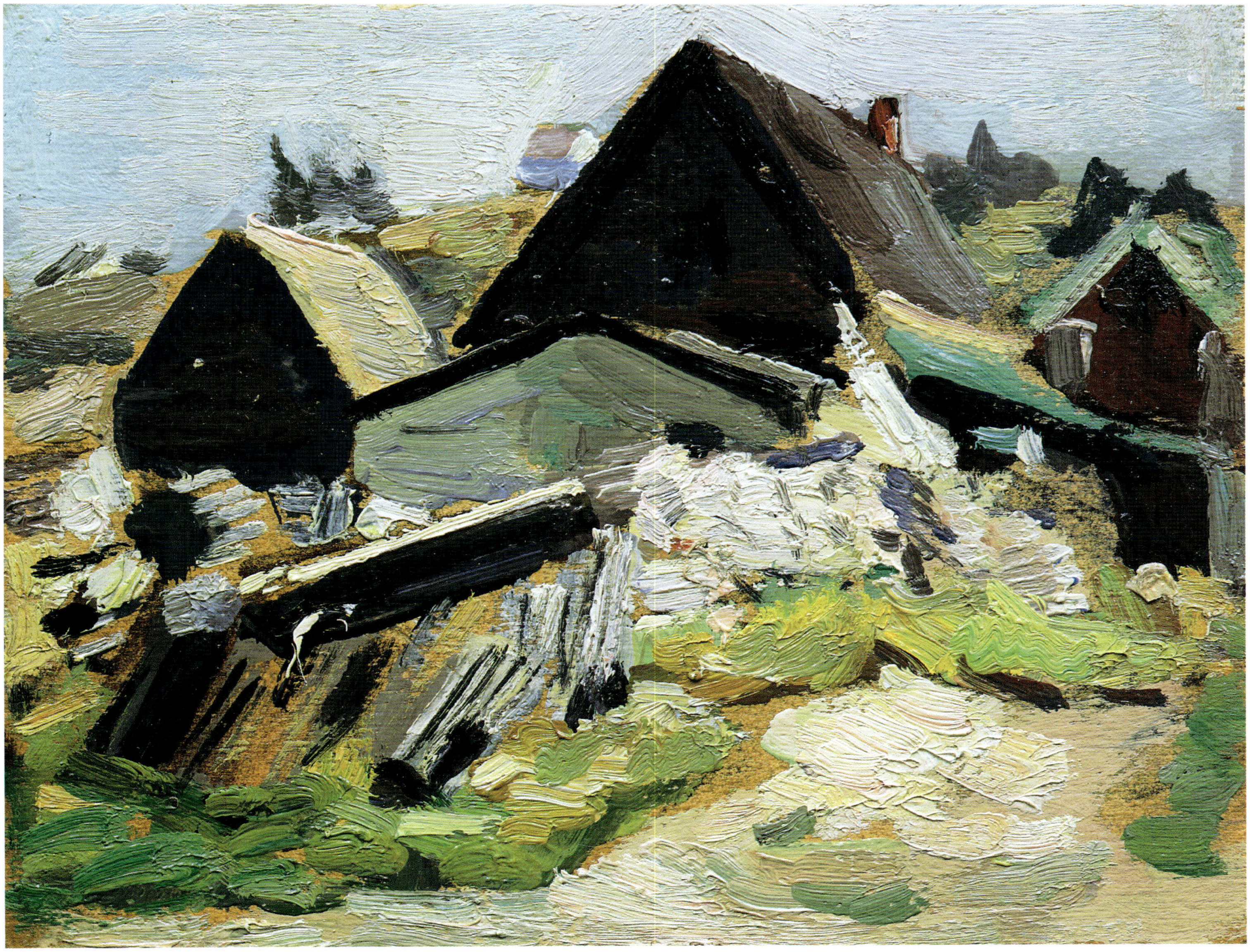

17.

Late Afternoon, 1934

Oil on canvas
30 × 36⅛ in. (76.2 × 91.7 cm)
Signed and dated lower left: *A. J. Bogdanove 1934*
Inscribed on verso: *Late Afternoon*

Portraying a span of rocks and sea, *Late Afternoon* simultaneously captures the concrete reality of a place and abstract issues of composition. This clearly legible image is also a virtuoso exercise in building a composition with two complementary colors—the palette is dominated by blue and orange tonalities and the neutral gray that they create in combination. As paintings like *Late Afternoon* demonstrate, Bogdanove perceived changing light and weather as springboards for exploring harmony, balance, and movement through the use of color.

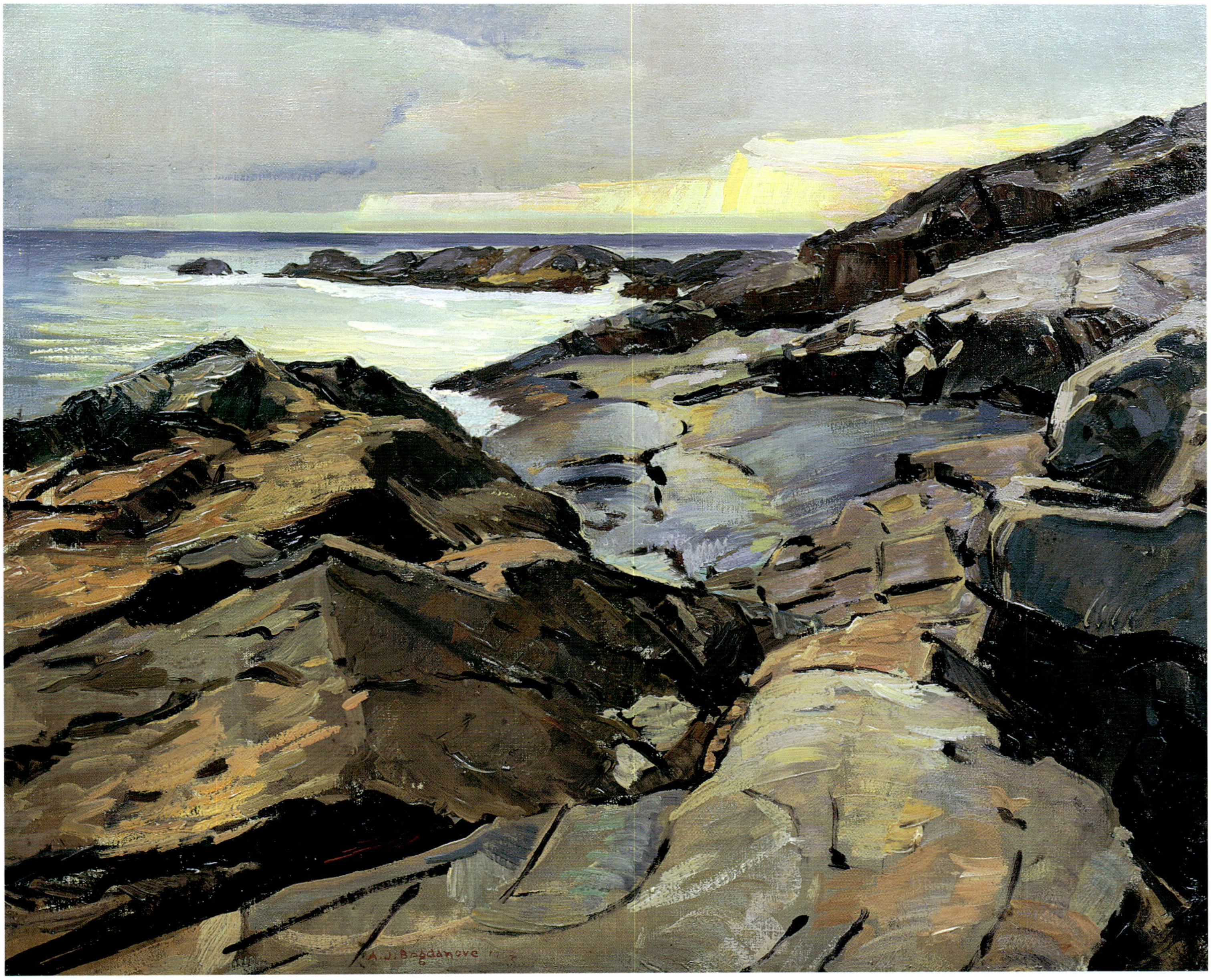
A. J. Bogdanove

18.

Boat Builders, ca. 1930–1940

Oil on board
9⅞ × 12 in. (25 × 30.5 cm)
Signed lower right: *A. J. Bogdanove*

Boat Builders is related to Bogdanove's *Fish Beach, Noon* (ca. 1930–1940; Monhegan Museum, Maine). Both paintings show workmen taking midday breaks in the summer sun, and with just a few swift strokes, Bogdanove perfectly evokes the men's relaxation and easy rapport. Although the sea is not depicted, its presence is strongly felt in the breezy ambiance of the painting, and in the subject of Fish Beach, which was an important working and gathering place for the fishermen on the island.

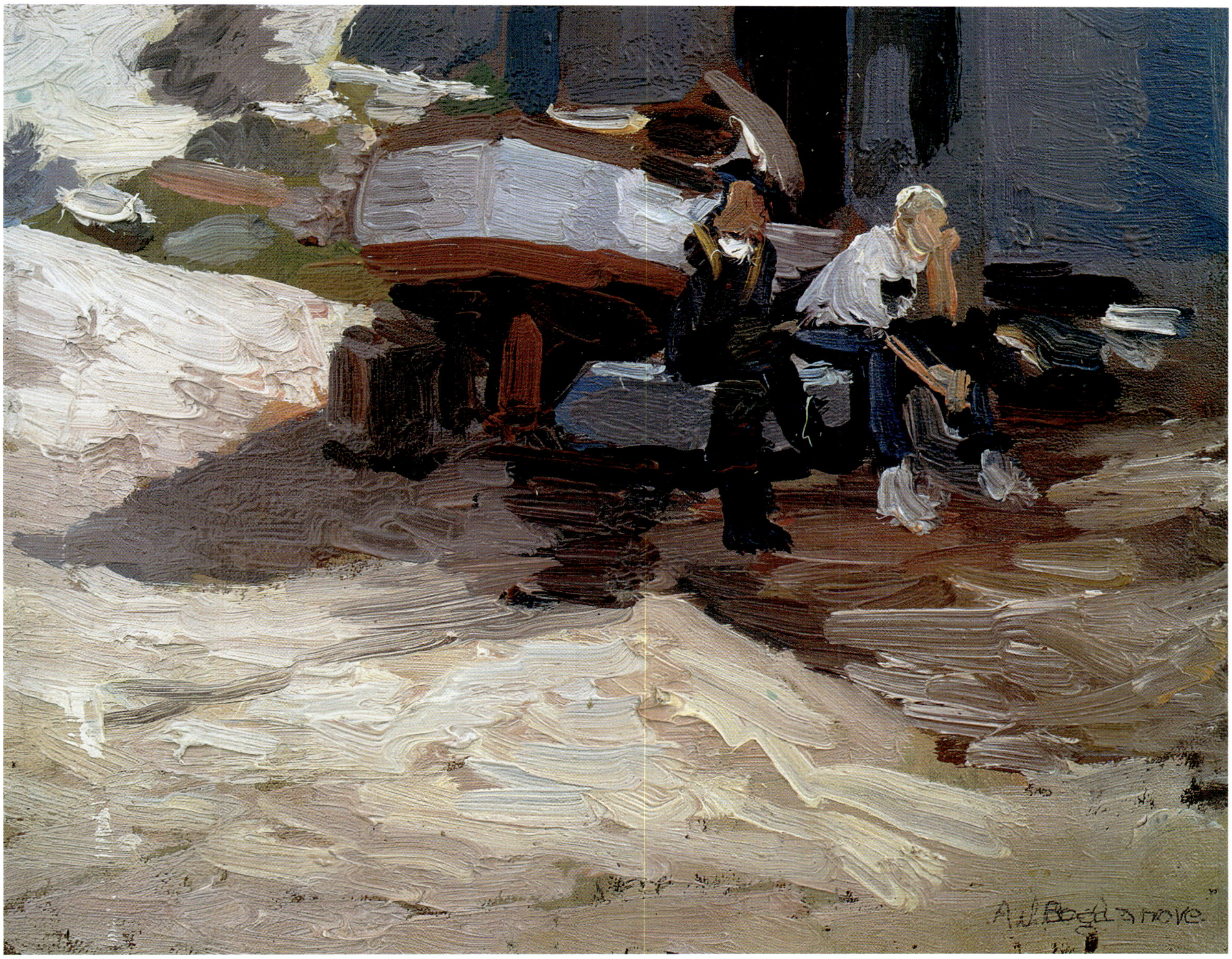
A.W. Bogdanove

19.

Little White Head, ca. 1920–1935

Oil on board
20 × 24 in. (50.8 × 61 cm)
Signed lower right: *A. J. Bogdanove*
Inscribed on verso: *Little Whitehead*

Bogdanove was endlessly fascinated by Monhegan Island's monumental rock formations and sought to convey their power and solidity in his paintings. In *Little White Head,* he portrayed one of the headlands on the eastern, or ocean, side of the island. Standing at the base of the cliff, he focused on the rocks before him, revealing his interest in exploring the way that sunlight cast polychrome reflections on their faceted surfaces.

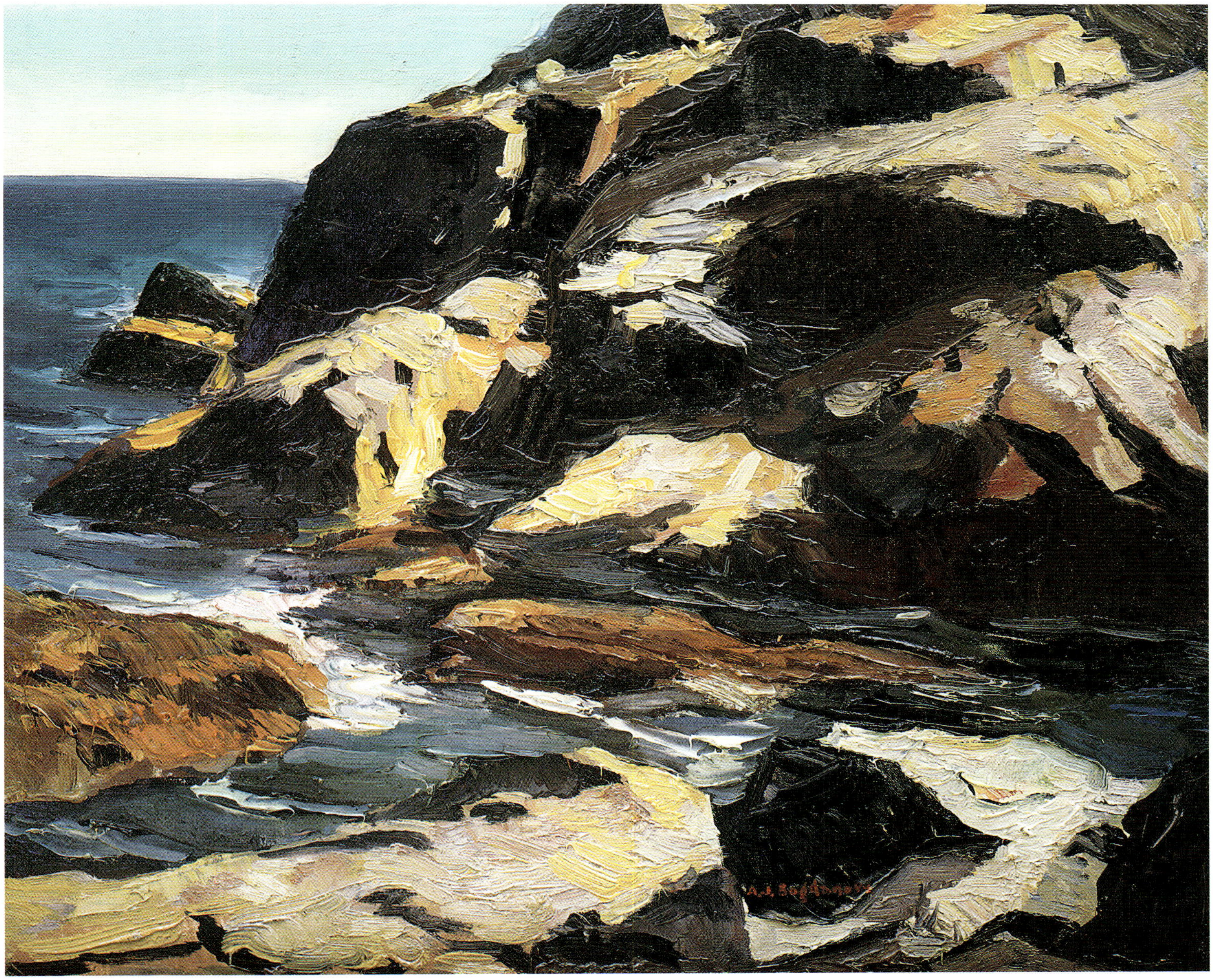

20.

Portrait of Mrs. W. (The Artist's Wife), ca. 1920

Oil on canvas
36 × 38 in. (91.4 × 96.5 cm)
Signed lower right: *A. J. Bogdanove*

In *Portrait of Mrs. W. (The Artist's Wife),* Bogdanove portrayed Pearl Winton, a former student whom he married in approximately 1920. The work was included in the artist's first solo exhibition, held in 1920 at the Young Men's Hebrew Association in New York. In the painting, Bogdanove depicts his wife seated on the front porch of the couple's Monhegan home, with the entrance to the harbor and the tip of Manana Island visible in the background. The heightened color in this work suggests the influence of the Monhegan views painted by Rockwell Kent in the early 1900s.

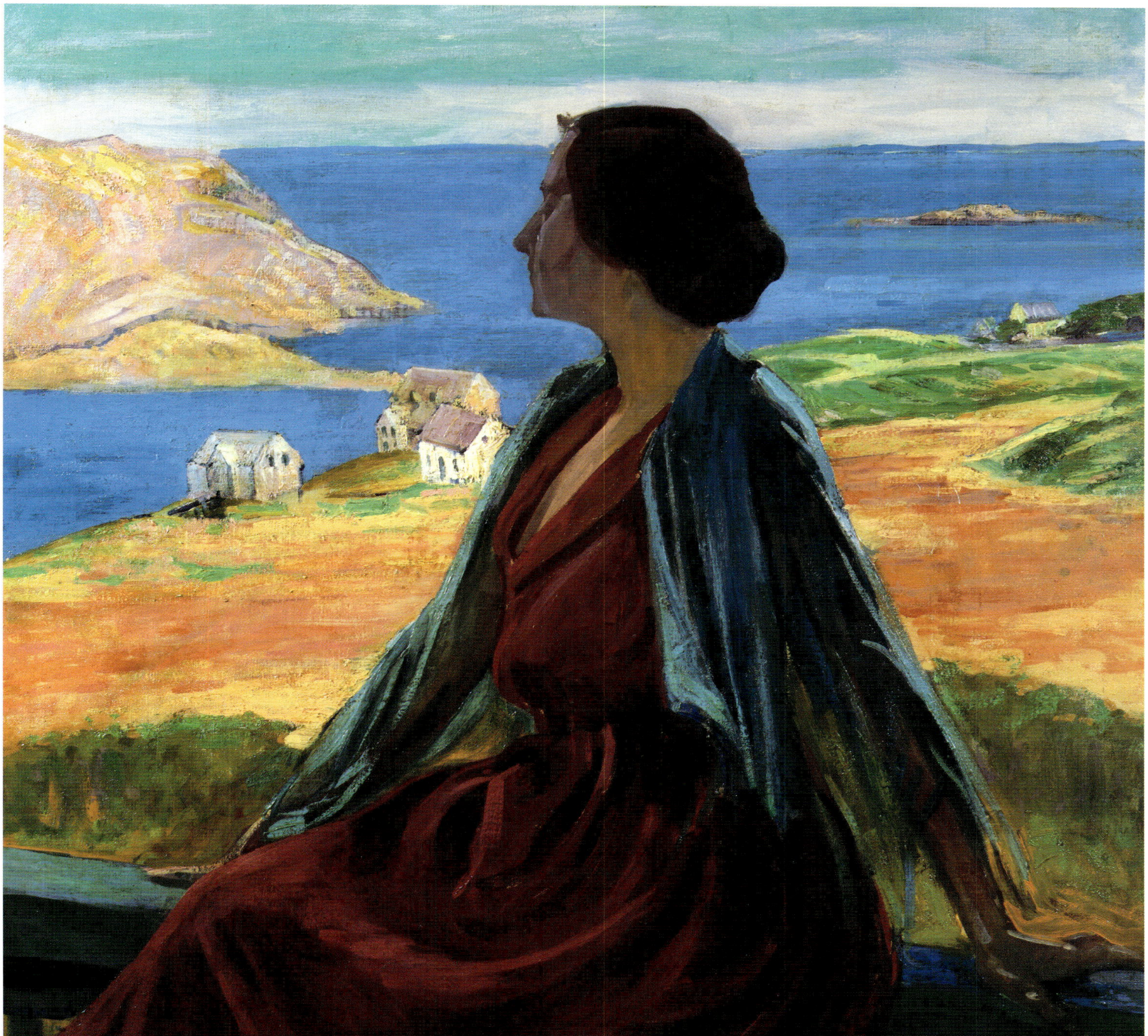

21.

Locomotive Rock, 1941

Oil on masonite

36 × 30 in. (91.4 × 76.2 cm)

Signed and dated lower left: *A.J. Bogdanove 1941*

In *Locomotive Rock,* Bogdanove depicted a rock formation that derived its name from its striking resemblance to the front of a locomotive. By painting the subject in shadow, Bogdanove heightened its similarity to a black, skirted train engine and emphasized the structure's mass. The imagery of a locomotive imparts a sense of propulsive force to this towering promontory of rock.

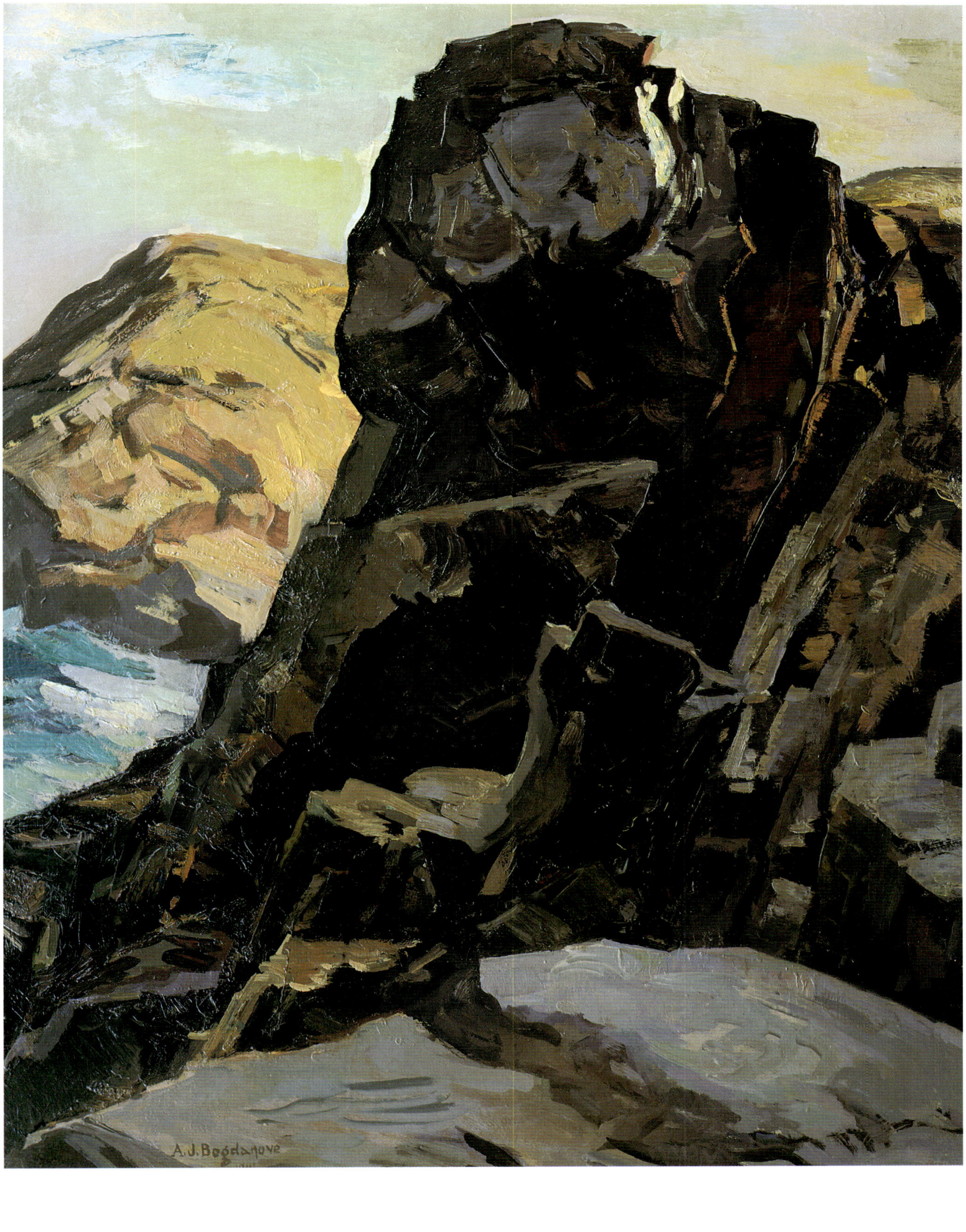
A.J. Bogdanove

22.

Monhegan Coast, ca. 1930–1940

Oil on canvas
25⅛ × 30 in. (63.8 × 76.2 cm)
Inscribed lower left: *A. J. Bogdanove*

Monhegan Coast offers a different angle on Monhegan's headlands than many of the artist's other images of them. Whereas Bogdanove often focused on the point where the craggy rock formations meet the sea, in this painting, he positioned himself at the top of the headlands, showing a cliff dropping precipitously away from the blanket of green at its summit. By depicting the rock face in shadow, the mass and solidity of the headlands are accentuated.

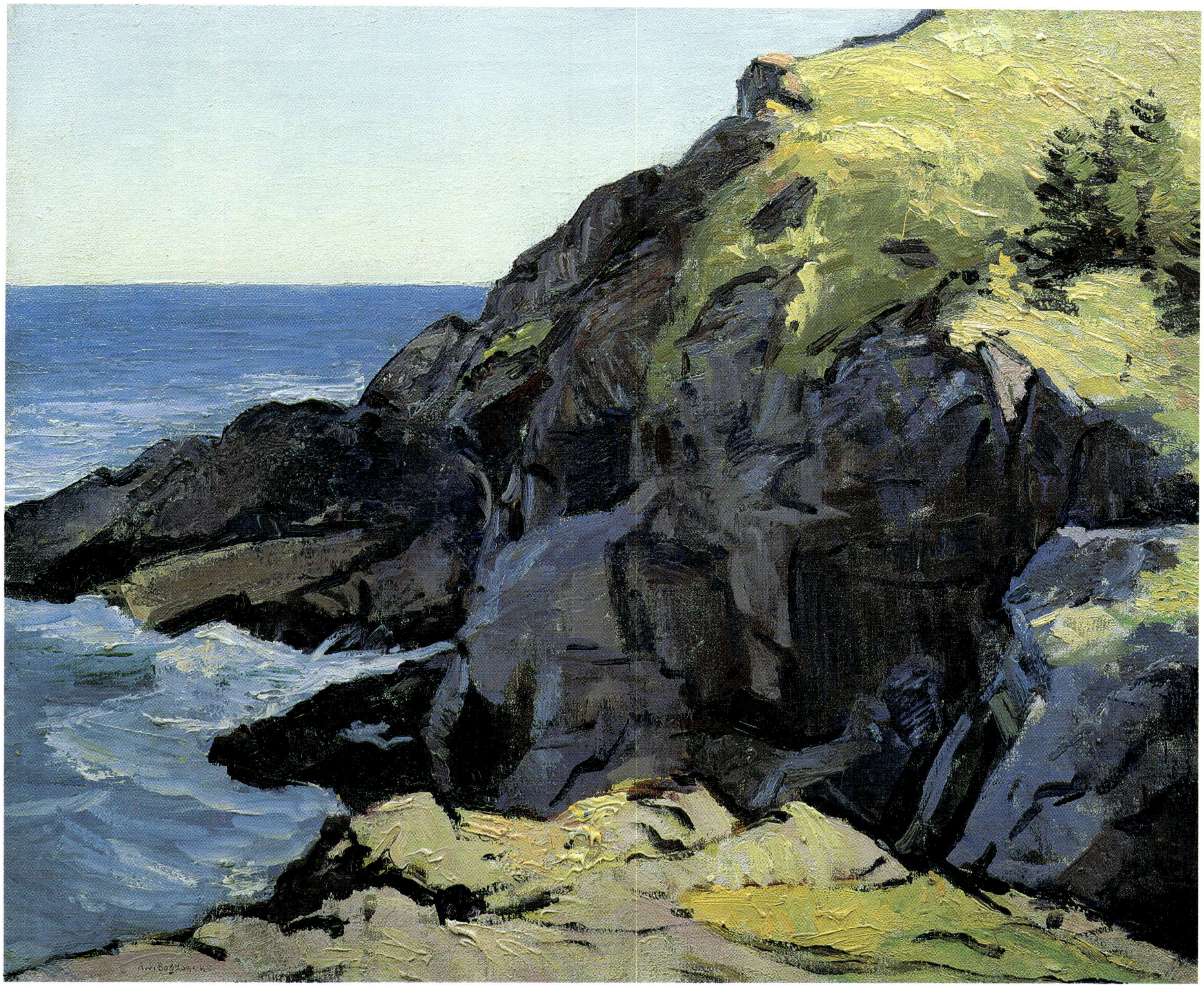

23.

Walter's Fish House, ca. 1920–1930

Oil on canvas
20 × 24 in. (50.8 × 61 cm)
Signed lower right: *A. J. Bogdanove*
Inscribed on verso: *Walters Fish House*

The house depicted in this work belonged to Walter Davis and stands beside Dwight Stanley's Fish House on Monhegan's harbor. Here, Bogdanove paints the view from the waterfront, framing the building against the rising hillside in the background. As in so many of the artist's landscapes, a sense of space is created by the relative position of the objects in the picture plane.

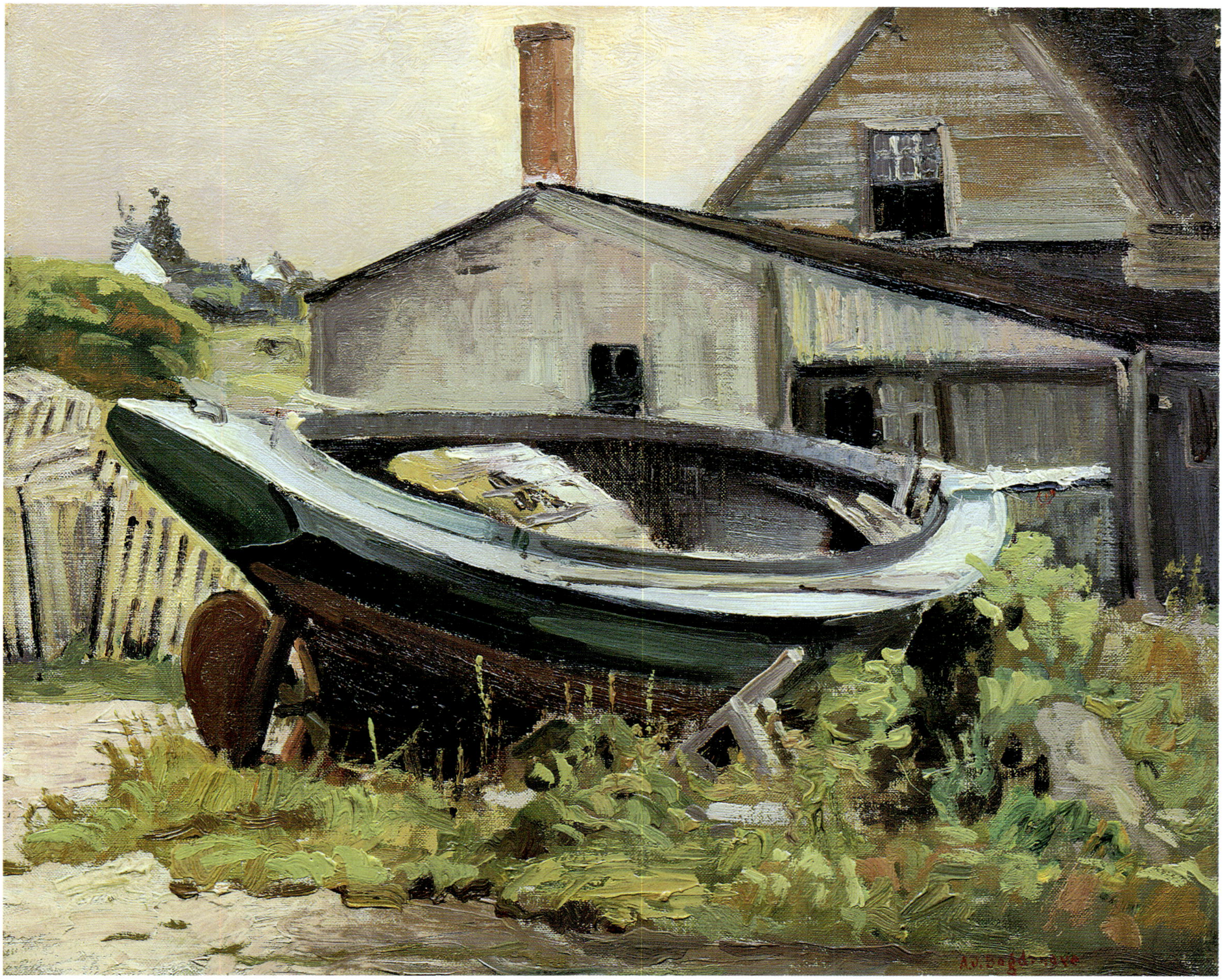

24.

Low Tide, ca. 1930–1935

Oil on canvas

25 × 30 in. (63.5 × 76.2 cm)

Signed lower right: *A. J. Bogdanove*

Inscribed on verso: *Low Tide*

An astute observer of Bogdanove's paintings noted in 1930 that his marines often place greater emphasis on rocks than on the sea, writing that Bogdanove's canvases "are well ballasted with rock," and that "his hard, crisp strokes of pigment applied impasto show his determination to realize the solidity of stone."[1] This critic could have been describing *Low Tide,* in which Bogdanove portrayed a view of a rugged outcropping that surrounds a tidal pool, with a glimpse of the sea visible in the right distance.

1. "Canvases Well Ballasted," newspaper clipping dated November 12, 1930, in Cabot Album, vol. III, Part II, Monhegan Library, Monhegan, Maine.

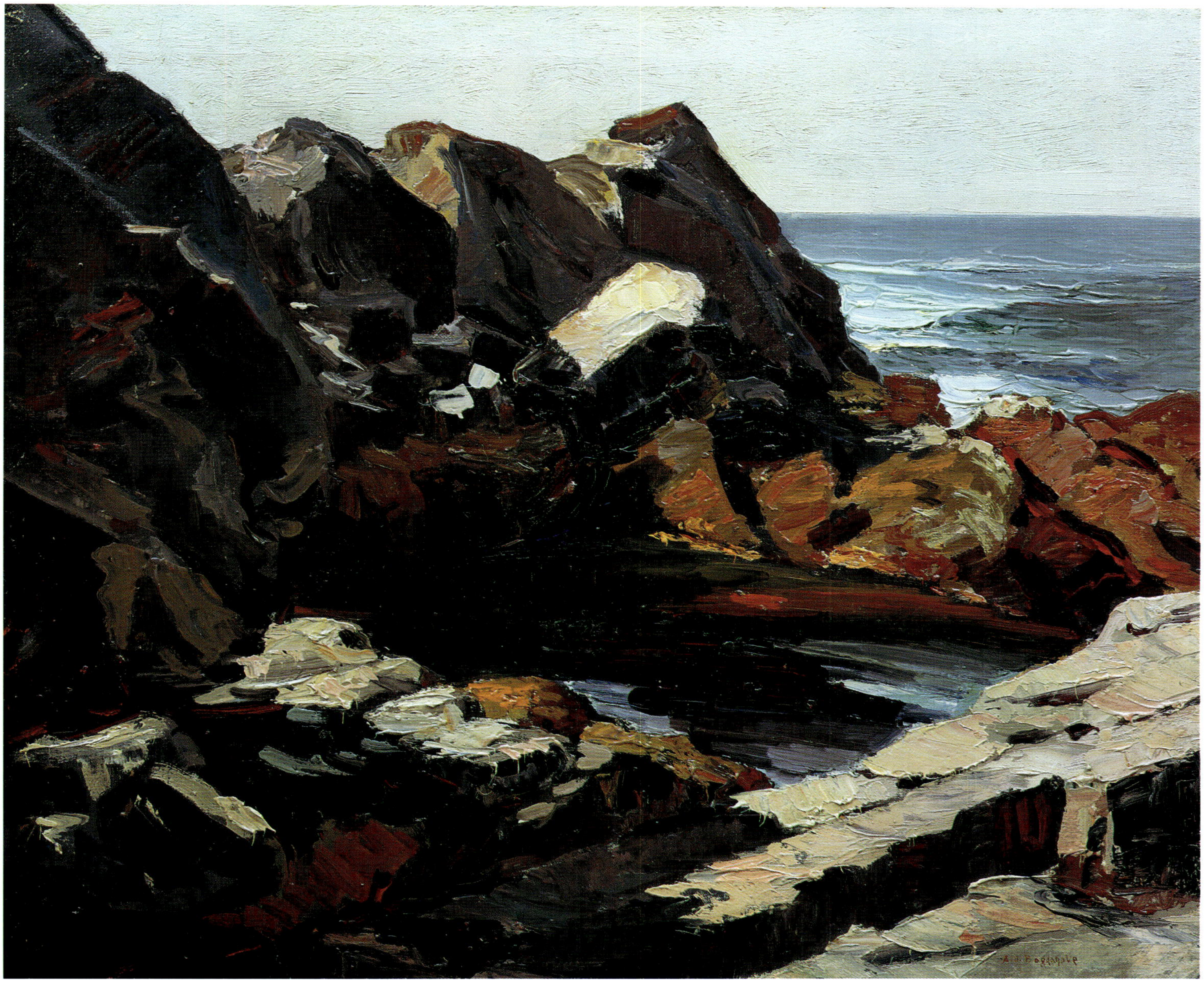

25.

Maine Road, ca. 1940–1945

Oil on board
9 × 12 in. (22.9 × 30.5 cm)
Signed lower right: *A. J. Bogdanove*

Throughout his career, Bogdanove painted large canvases directly from nature, but he also often executed quick portable studies known as *pochades*, which allowed him to work with great ease and spontaneity. His vigorous approach is demonstrated in *Maine Road*. The saturated tones of ochre, green, teal, and gray in this work reveal that it was created by Bogdanove late in his career, when he returned to the more Impressionist brushwork typical of his earliest landscapes, but worked with a boldness and assuredness that reflect his artistic maturity.

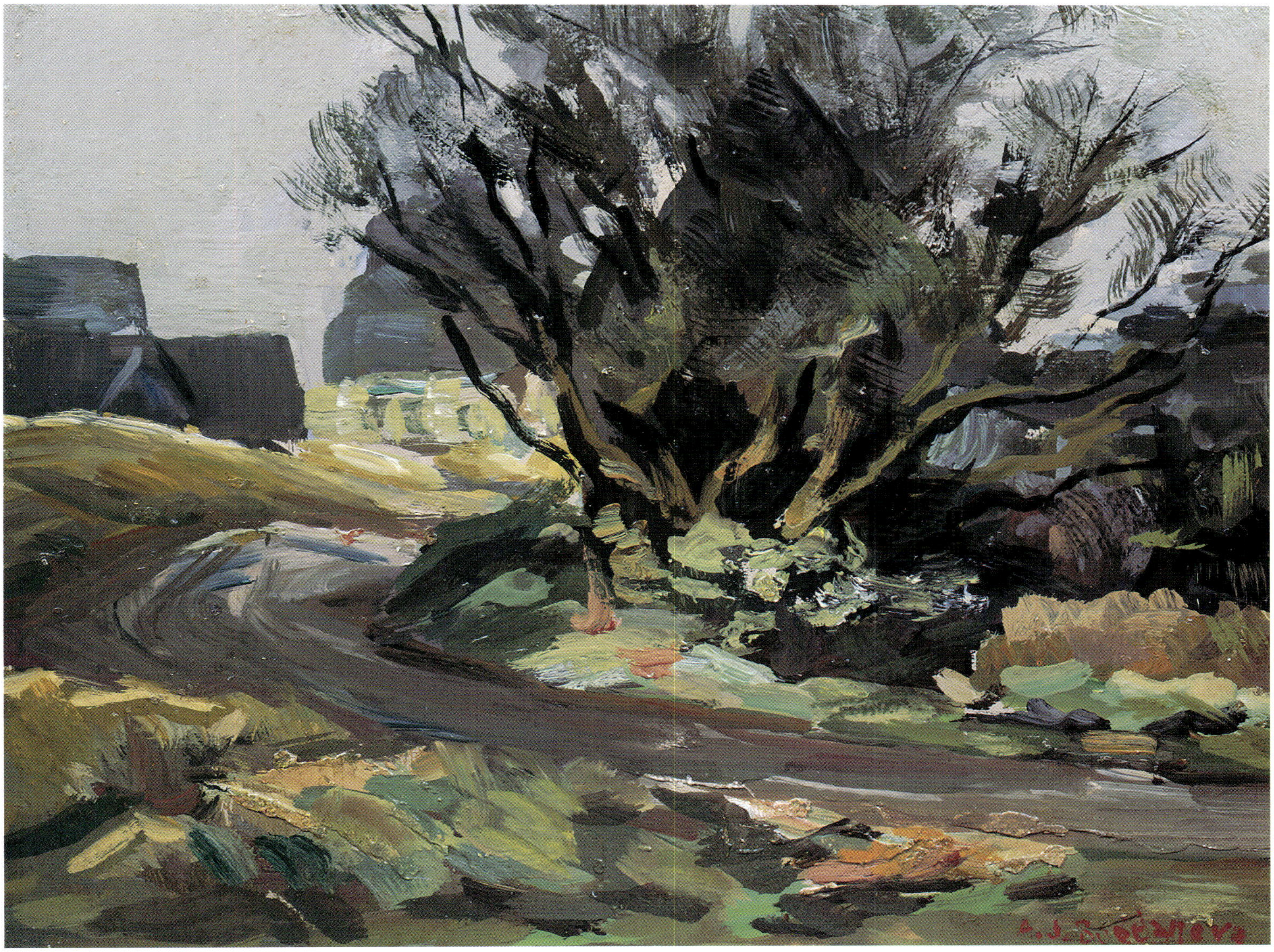

26.

Fog Horn Station, Manana, ca. 1930–1935

Oil on masonite
18 × 24 in. (45.7 × 61 cm)
Signed lower right: *A. J. Bogdanove*
Inscribed on verso: *Fog Horn Station*

The fog signal that serves Monhegan Island is located on the mainland side of Manana Island. While not visible from Monhegan, its horn is omnipresent. Both Robert Henri and George Bellows complained to their families about its incessant moan during stretches of bad weather. Nonetheless, many artists considered the station to be highly picturesque. Bogdanove painted the subject at least twice, both times from this dramatic perspective at the base of Manana. In *Fog Horn Station,* he used a low vantage point to capture the dramatic spectacle of the station perched on a cliff of sun-bleached rocks. His image of crisply defined architectural structures standing precariously on a cliff is, in fact, close in spirit to Edward Hopper's 1927–1929 images of Lighthouse Hill on Cape Elizabeth, Maine, such as *Lighthouse at Two Lights* (1929; Metropolitan Museum of Art, New York).

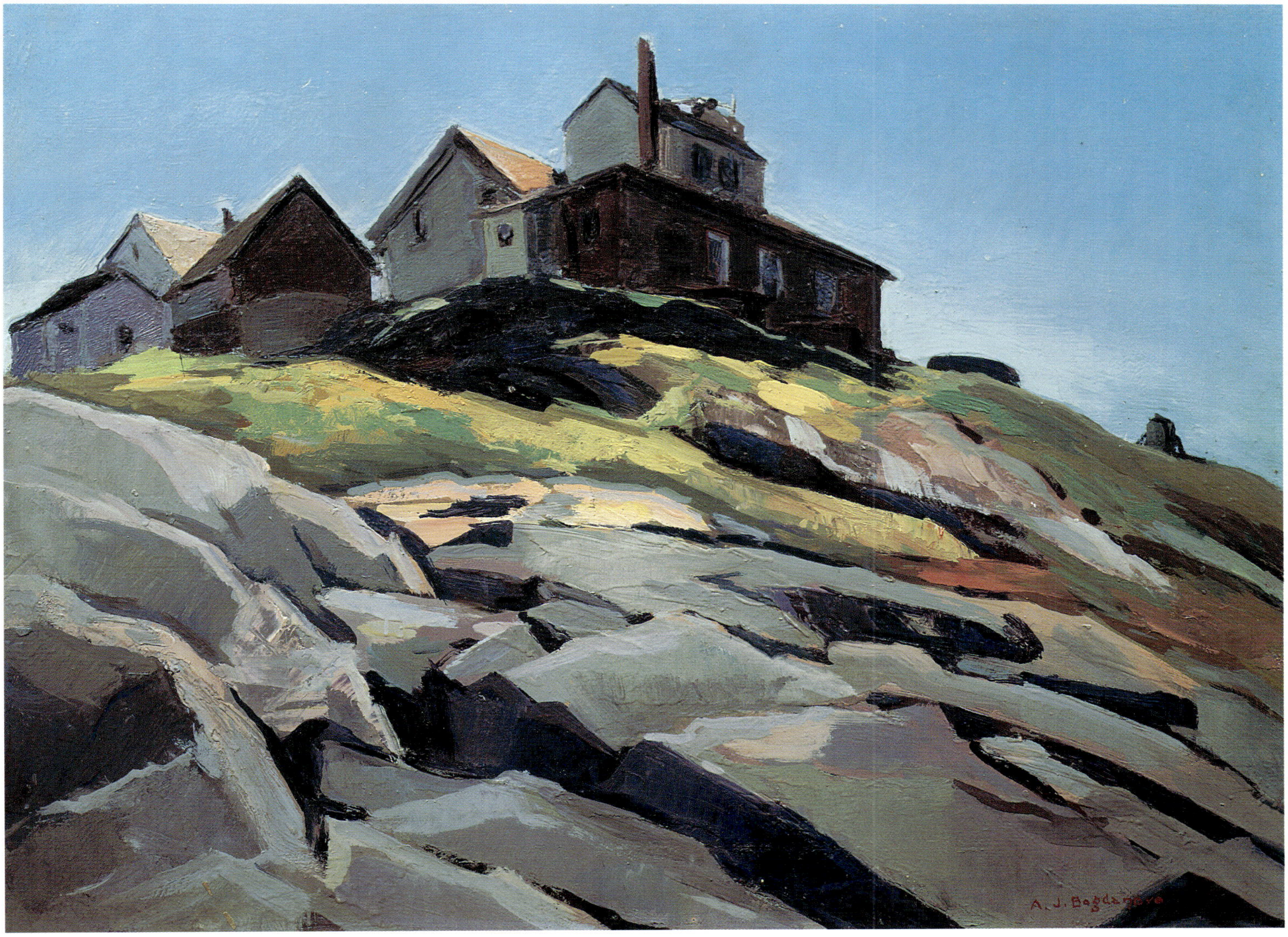
A. J. Bogdanove

27.

Sunset, ca. 1925–1935

Oil on canvas

25 × 30 in. (63.5 × 76.2 cm)

Signed lower right: *A. J. Bogdanove*

Inscribed on verso: *Sunset*

In most of his works, Bogdanove featured landscapes seen in bright sunlight, but he also painted at transitional times of day, studying changing effects of light. In *Sunset,* he observed the impact of the sun setting behind Manana Island. The work was painted from the northern end of Monhegan looking toward the two small islands, known together as Smutty Nose, which are situated at the entrance to the harbor, west of Monhegan. The boathouse seen on Manana's shore is depicted in a closer view in Bogdanove's *The Harbor* (pl. 6). In the scene, Bogdanove brings out the harmonious range of lavender and silvery gray tonalities that were the result of subdued light conditions as the day was reaching its end, and he took note especially of the way that the dark form of Manana was strongly silhouetted against a glowing sky.

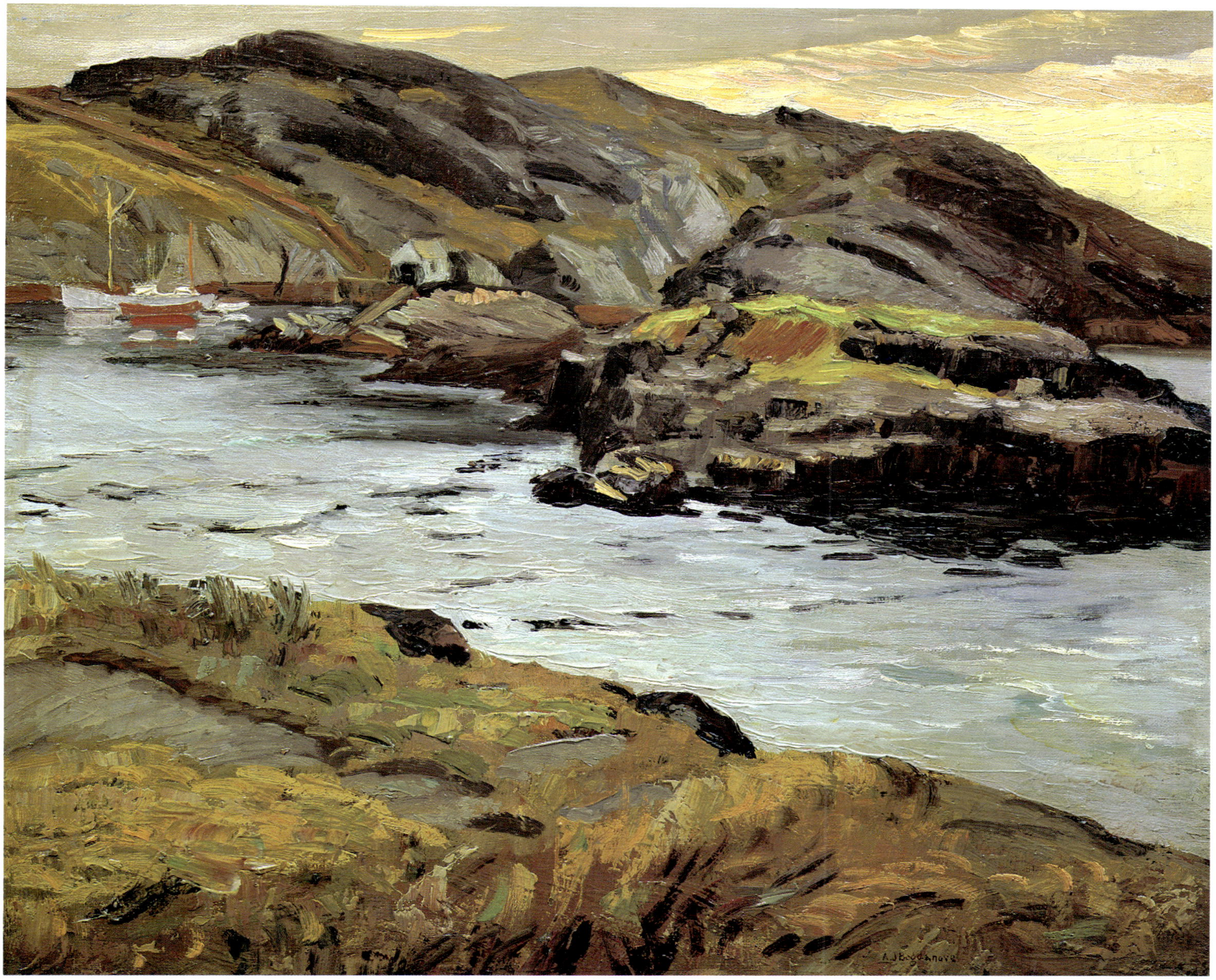

28.

The Squall, ca. 1933–1938

Oil on canvasboard
18 × 24 in. (45.7 × 61 cm)
Signed lower right: *A. J. Bogdanove*
Inscribed on verso: *The Squall*

Bogdanove was fascinated by the curves of hulls, especially those of sturdy fishing vessels; consequently, he painted boats drawn up on shore more often than out on the water. *The Squall* is an animated portrayal of a boat resting on one of Monhegan's harbor front beaches, framed against the silhouette of the wharf and the buildings rising up from the landing. This perspective on the harbor was a favorite of artist Randall Davey's when he was on Monhegan in the 1910s. In *The Squall,* Bogdanove portrayed his subject with especially crisp brushwork, heightening the contrast between the warm sunlight on the beach and the dark shadowed form of the landed boat.

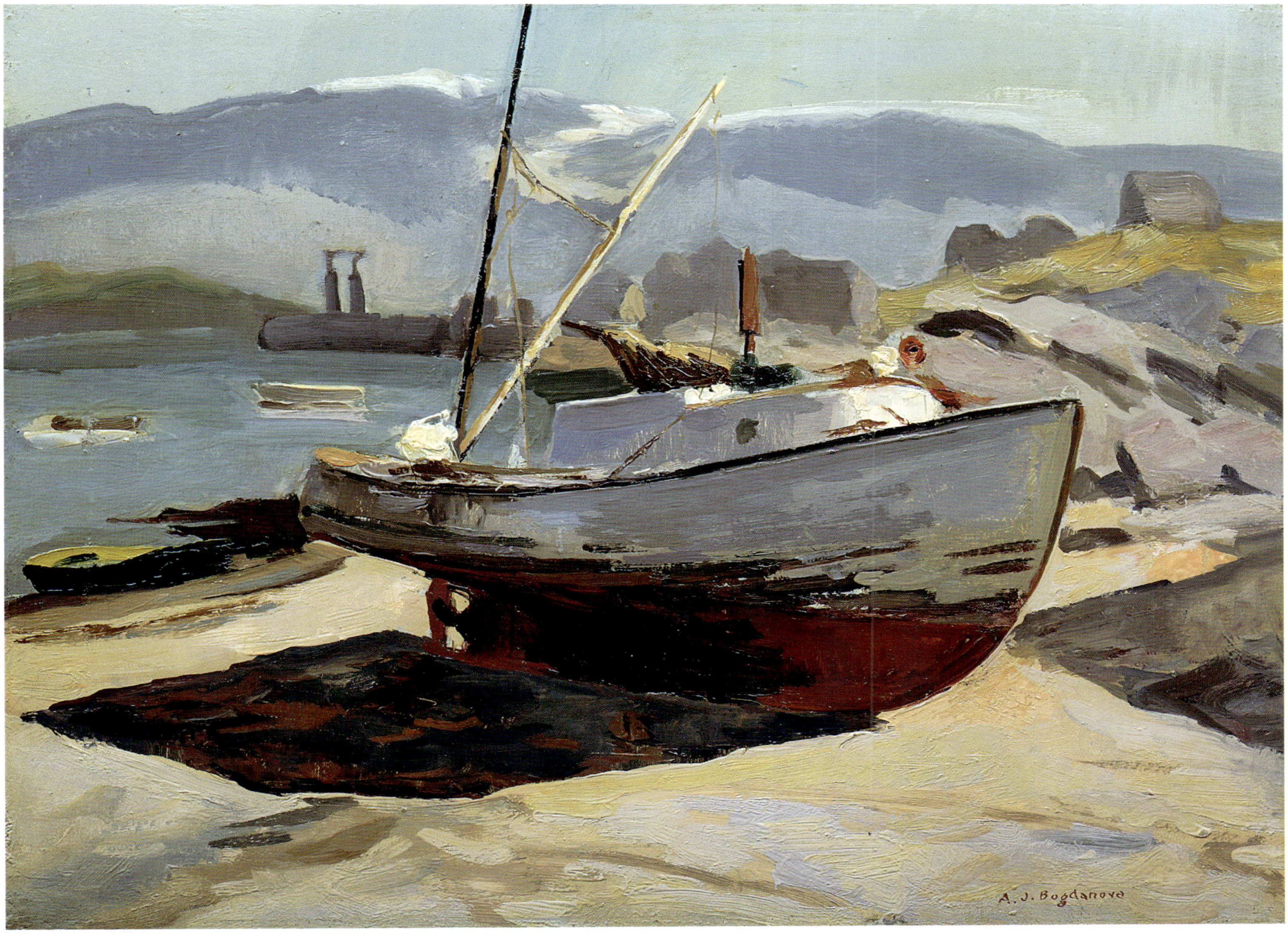
A. J. Bogdanove

29.

Scotty Painting, ca. 1915–1930

Oil on canvas
20 × 24 in. (50.8 × 61 cm)
Inscribed on verso: *Scotty Painting*

By contrast with many of Bogdanove's works which convey a feeling of solitude, *Scotty Painting* evokes the camaraderie of artists working together. Perhaps executed in the meadow on Horn's Hill, just below Bogdanove's Monhegan studio, this painting offers a glimpse of Bogdanove's approach. In the painting, an artist wearing a beret is shown directly facing the sunlight, while his easel is shielded from the glare of the sun's rays. Bogdanove's broad, assured brushstrokes show his gift for quickly capturing the salient qualities of a landscape as well as an individual's stance and gestures.

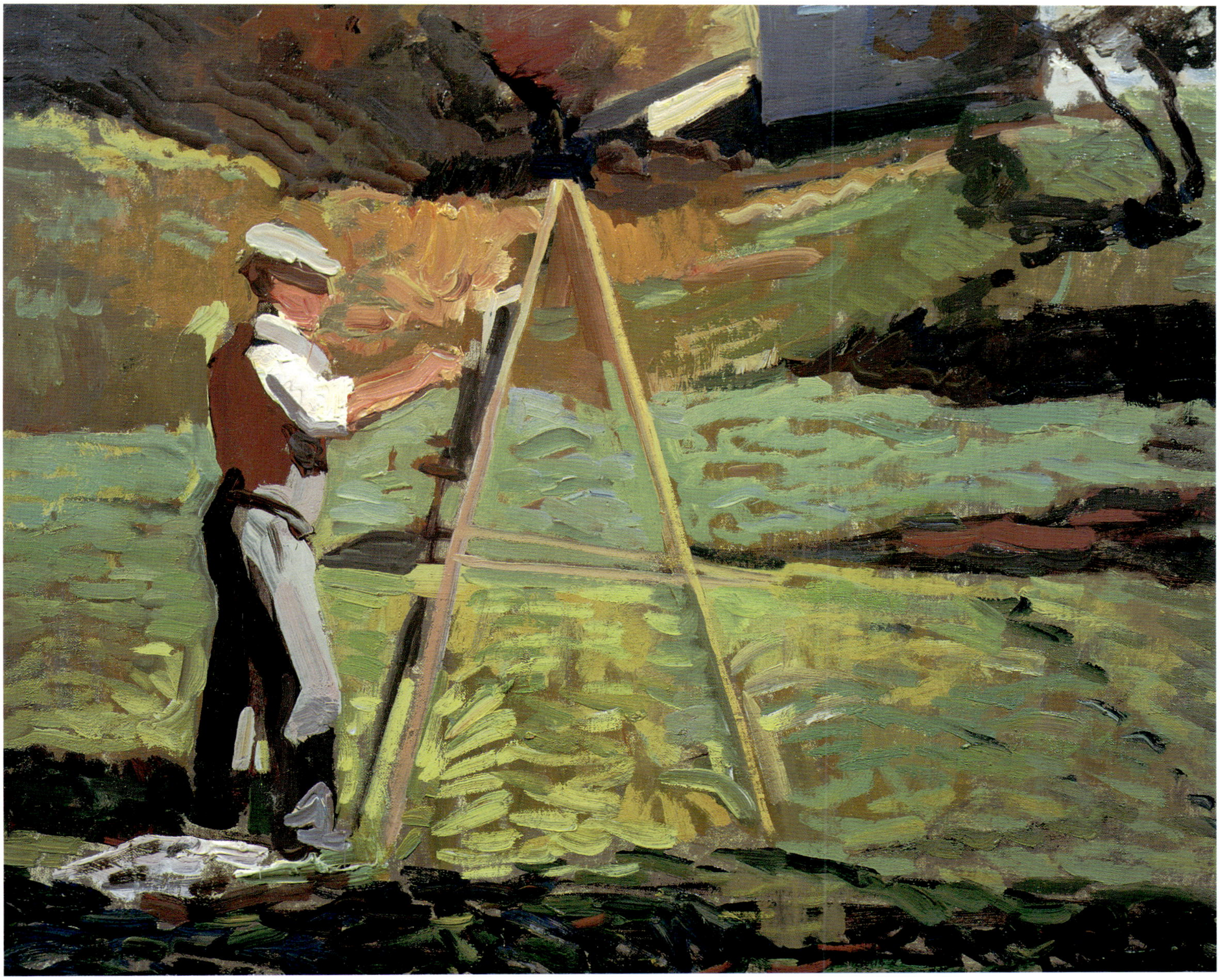

30.

Ami, ca. 1925–1935

Oil on board
12 × 15⅞ in. (30.5 × 40.2 cm)
Inscribed on verso: *Ami*

Although Bogdanove was active as a portraitist, he only occasionally painted figurative pictures during his summers in Maine. The subject in *Ami* was probably a friend from the island's community of artists or possibly one of Bogdanove's summer students. Using somber tones to portray rocks and water and an especially vigorous brush handling in the sea and sky, this panel recalls the Monhegan paintings created by George Bellows in the previous decade.

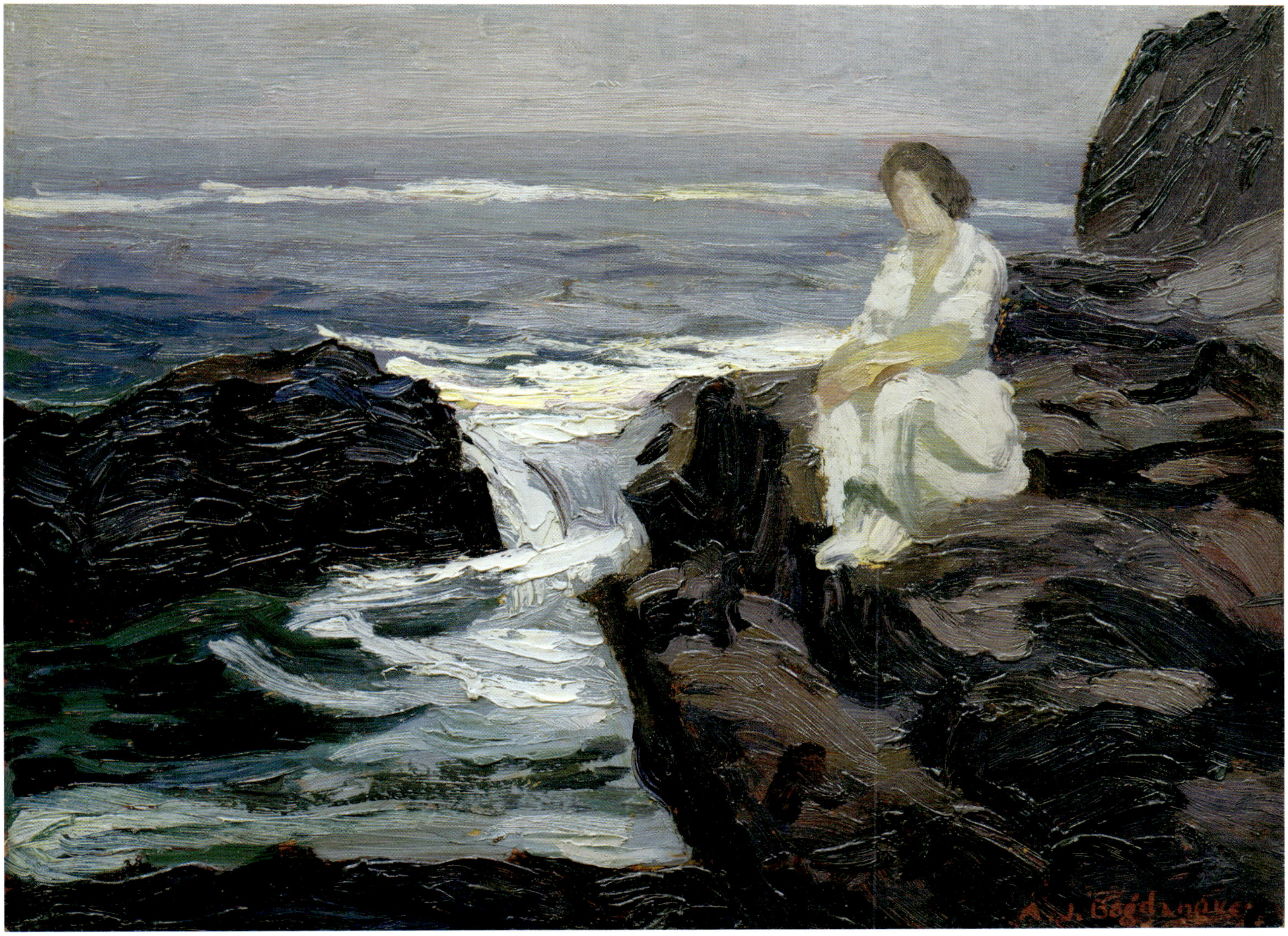

31.

Oceanside, ca. 1925–1935

Oil on canvasboard
12 × 16 in. (30.5 × 40.6 cm)
Signed lower right: *A. J. Bogdanove*

Bogdanove was not especially interested in sweeping panoramas; instead he preferred to focus on particular aspects of sites, often showing his motifs from low vantage points. Featuring a rocky outcropping seen on a diagonal within a tightly cropped image, *Oceanside* is characteristic of his Monhegan art. The painting is reminiscent of the jewel-like panels painted by Robert Henri on Monhegan in 1911, and like Henri, Bogdanove used a palette dominated by greens, grays and browns, bold, energetic brushwork, and a composition that is quite abstract.

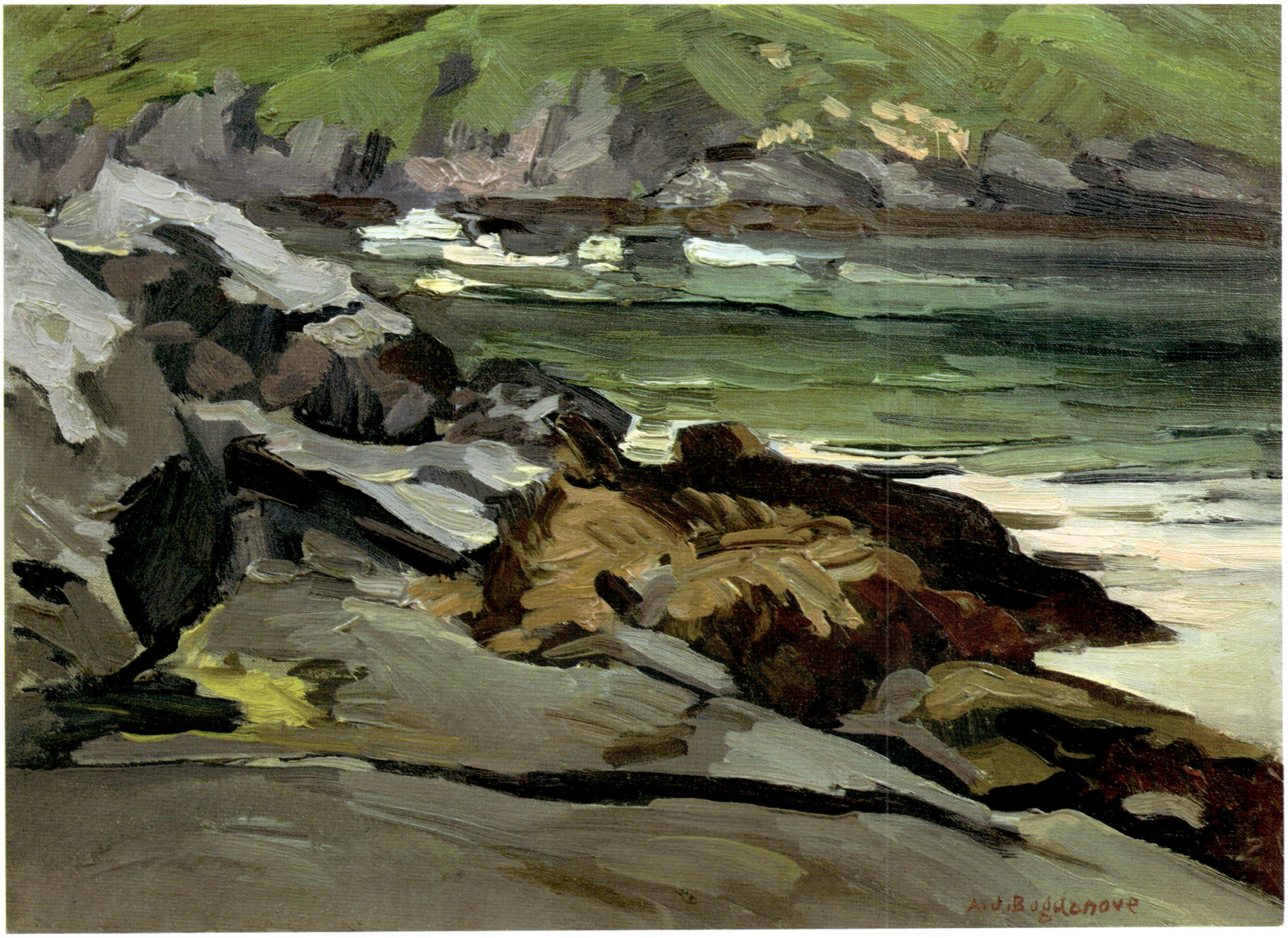
A.J.Bogdanove

32.

Fish Houses, Monhegan, ca. 1925–1935

Oil on canvas
30 × 36 in. (76.2 × 91.4 cm)

In *Fish Houses, Monhegan,* Bogdanove provides a broad view of Monhegan's harbor front fish houses, revealing the relationships between buildings, which are depicted in detail in his other works such as *Fish Shack and Lobster Pots* (pl. 43). Here Bogdanove's use of bright greens and purple-grays and his vigorous handling of paint recall the best of George Bellows's 1913 Monhegan paintings.

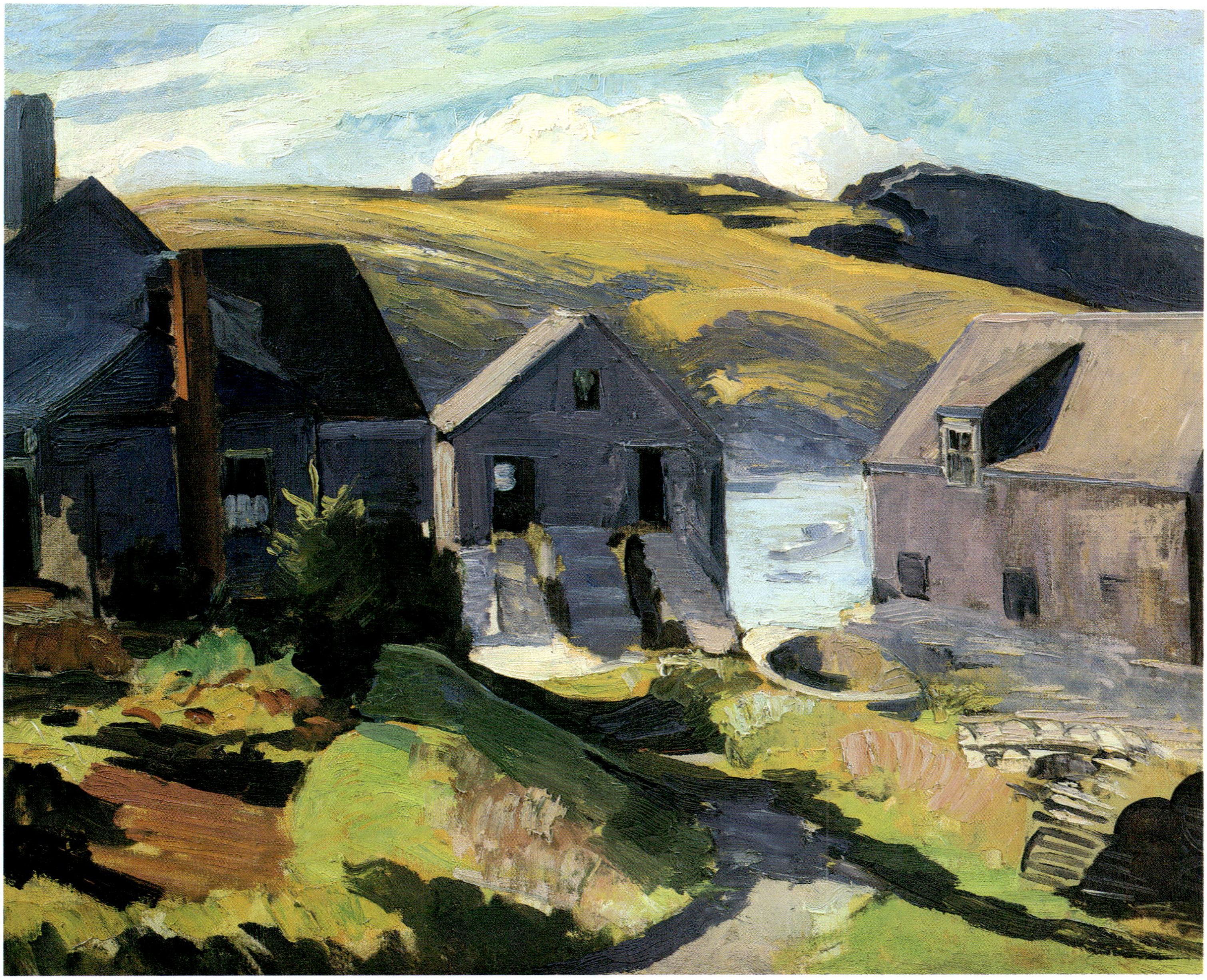

33.

Boat and Boathouse, ca. 1935–1945

Oil on canvas
29⅞ × 36 in. (75.8 × 91.4 cm)

Whereas many artists who painted on Monhegan featured primarily scenes of sunny days, the fog and violent storms typical of the island's weather inspired many of Bogdanove's best works. Indeed, titles of Bogdanove's paintings listed in exhibition catalogues such as *Gull Rock in Fog, The Fog Bow, Monhegan in Fog,* and *In Fog,* demonstrate his interest in capturing Monhegan's sites in what might be considered adverse conditions. His approach is demonstrated in *Boat and Boathouse,* where he took advantage of the soft, diffuse quality of Monhegan's light on a hazy day. He captures the way that the forms of land and sea have become softly blurred, while the near forms of a beached boat and shed remain in crisp focus.

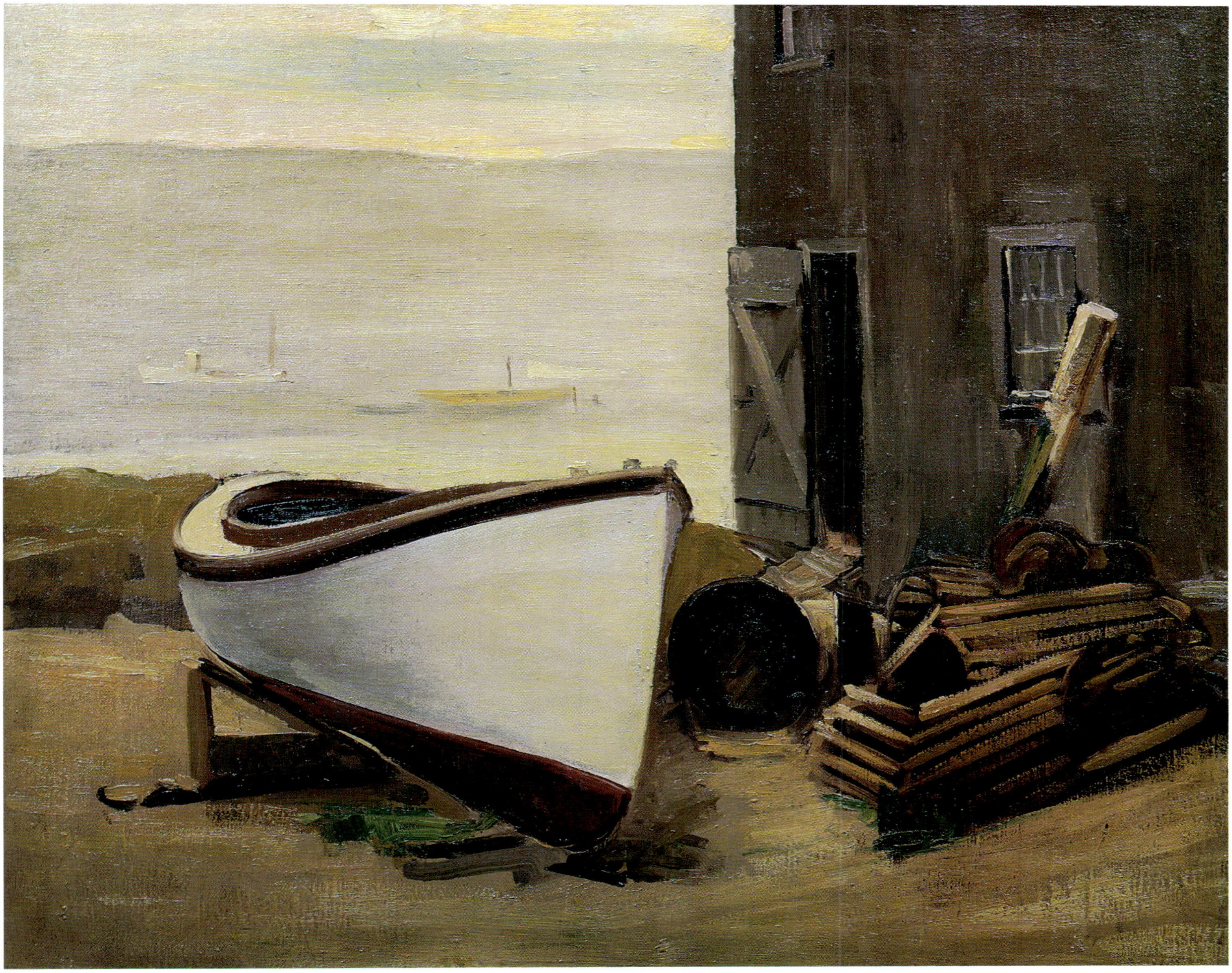

34.

Amoskeag Mills, Dunbarton, New Hampshire, ca. 1942–1946

Oil on board
18 × 24 in. (45.7 × 61 cm)
Signed lower right: *A. J. Bogdanove*
Inscribed on verso: *Amoskeag Mills*

Upon retiring in 1942 from his teaching position at the College of the City of New York (now City College of The City University of New York), Bogdanove moved from Manhattan to the small New Hampshire village of Dunbarton, near Manchester. Here he had year-round access to New England's landscape and could readily visit with his friend and fellow Monhegan painter Maude Briggs Knowlton, who was the director of the Currier Gallery in Manchester and had long been interested in his work.

At some point after his move, Bogdanove painted *Amoskeag Mills,* a view of the state's monumental textile mills. Instead of featuring the interior of the mill, Bogdanove chose to depict it from a distance, portraying its massive silhouette from across a stretch of snow-covered land, crossed by trickling brooks. One of only a few known winter scenes by the artist, this painting demonstrates Bogdanove's realist approach. The snow is wet and melting, rather than fresh and new. The whiteness of the ground cover offsets the drama of the mill, which seems to rise with the proud strength of one of Monhegan's rocky cliffs.

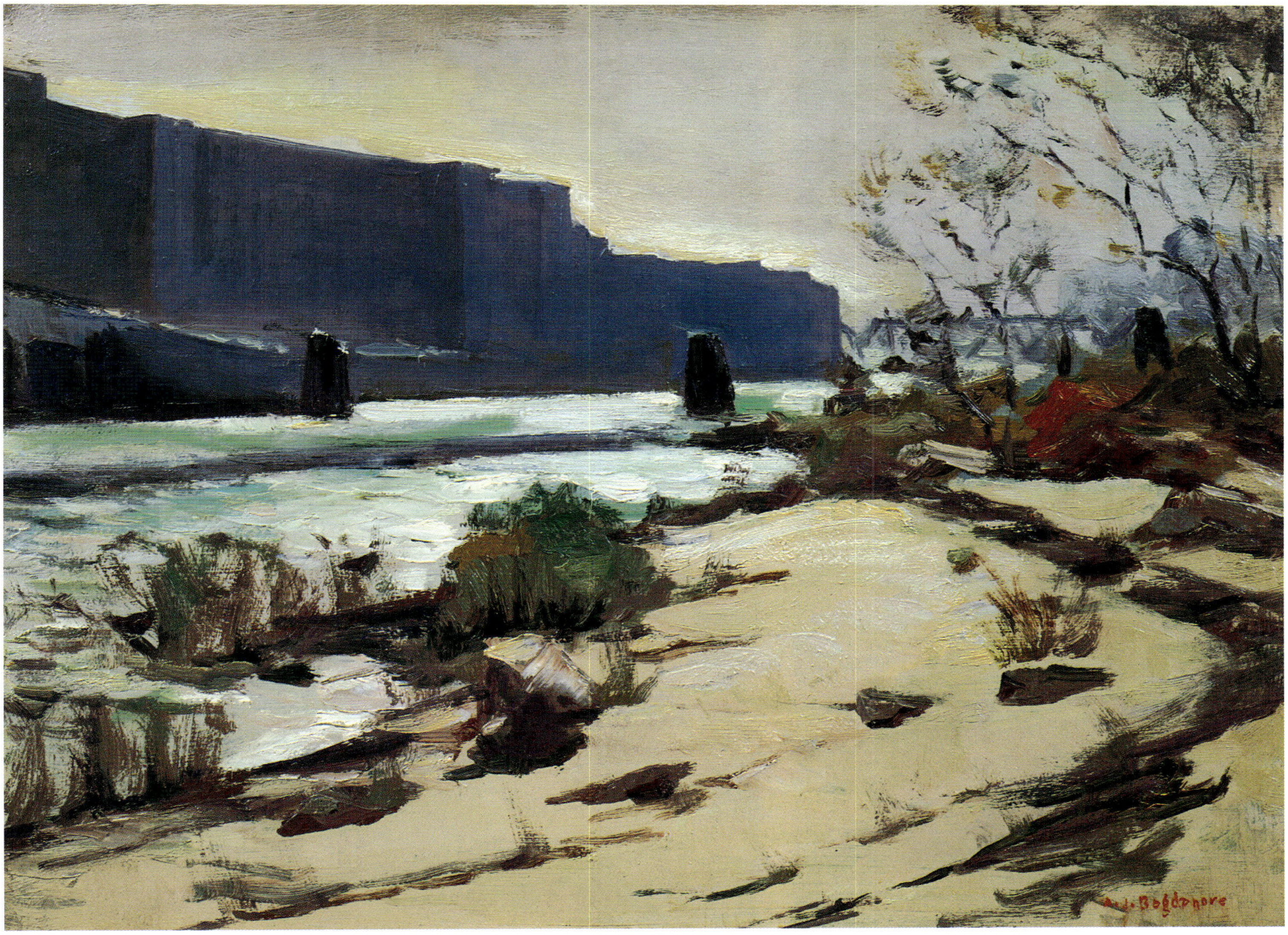

35.

From Manana, 1935

Oil on board
19⅞ × 24 in. (50.4 × 61 cm)
Signed lower right: *A. J. Bogdanove*
Inscribed on verso: *From Manana*

In *From Manana,* Bogdanove portrays a view looking back toward Monhegan from the crest of Manana Island. Most of Monhegan's harbor front is very low-lying, and therefore this is probably an image of the area known as Horn's Hill, which rises up to Manana's height. The development of Horn's Hill in the early twentieth century was concurrent with the first influx of artists on Monhegan, many of whom had studios there including Bogdanove. Although Bogdanove chose to feature the small clustered cottages that were typical of Horn's Hill, his own home is not depicted in this work.

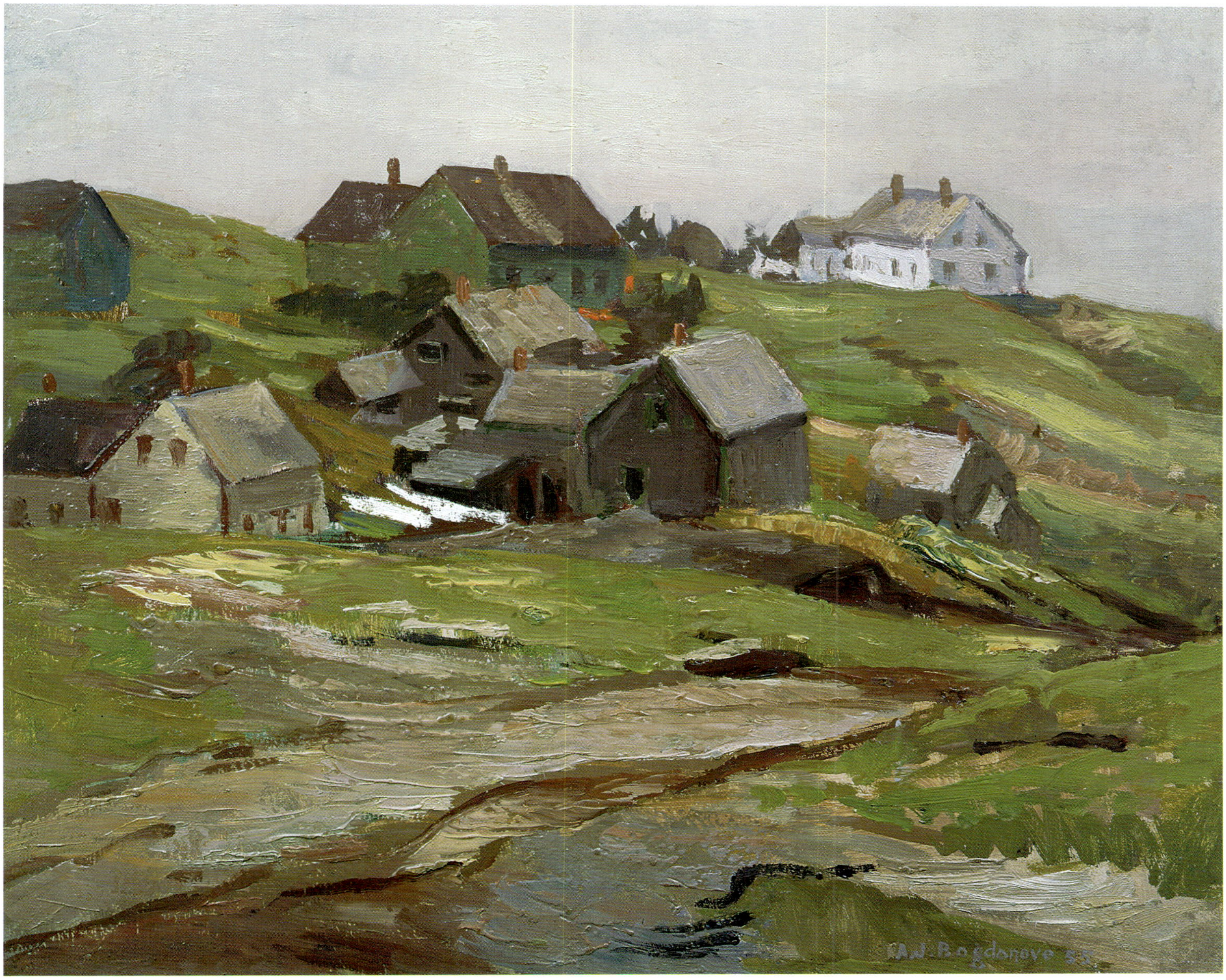
A.J. Bogdanove

36.

Lobster Cove, ca. 1938–1945

Oil on canvas
$29\frac{1}{4} \times 35\frac{7}{8}$ in. $(74.3 \times 91$ cm)
Inscribed on verso: *Lobster Cove*

Situated on the southern tip of Monhegan Island, Lobster Cove is the rocky point where the towering headlands on the eastern side of the island run gradually down to the ocean. In good or inclement weather, crashing waves can be found pounding against the rocky shore. The drama of this locale made it popular with many early twentieth-century painters including Robert Henri and George Bellows. For Bogdanove, the site was a favorite, and he portrayed it in some of his most powerful images that convey the sea's elemental force.

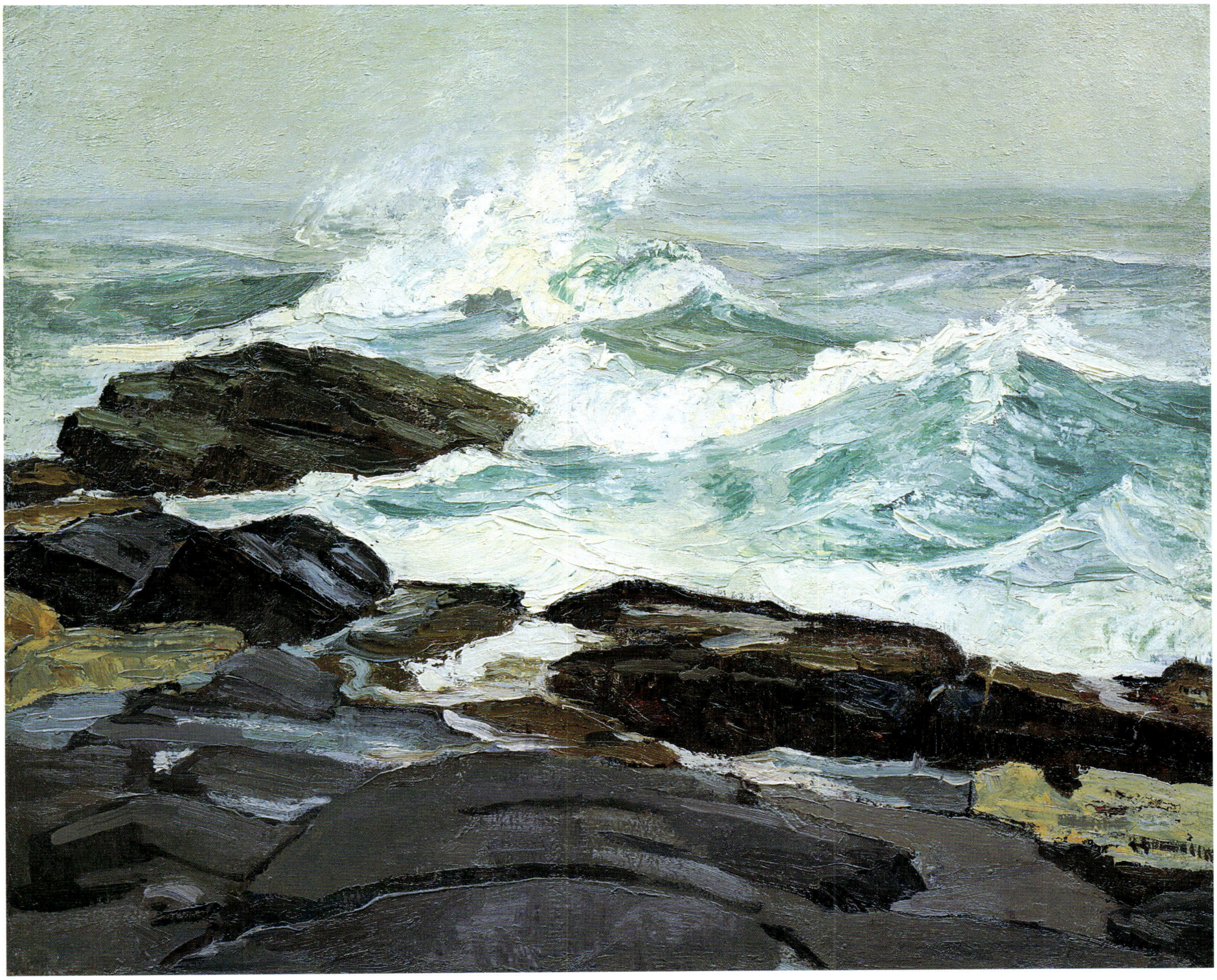

37.

Boats, ca. 1920–1930

Oil on canvas on board
11⅞ × 16 in. (30 × 40.6 cm)
Signed lower right: *A. J. Bogdanove*
Inscribed on verso: *Boats*

Using a rich, pastel palette and painting his subject with broad, swollen curves, in *Boats,* Bogdanove emulated the art of Eric Hudson, who was one of Monhegan Island's important artists in the first decades of the twentieth century. Hudson, who initially visited the island on a sailing trip in the 1890s, built a summer house on the harbor's edge. Here painters gathered nightly to offer critiques of each others' work and debate aesthetic issues.

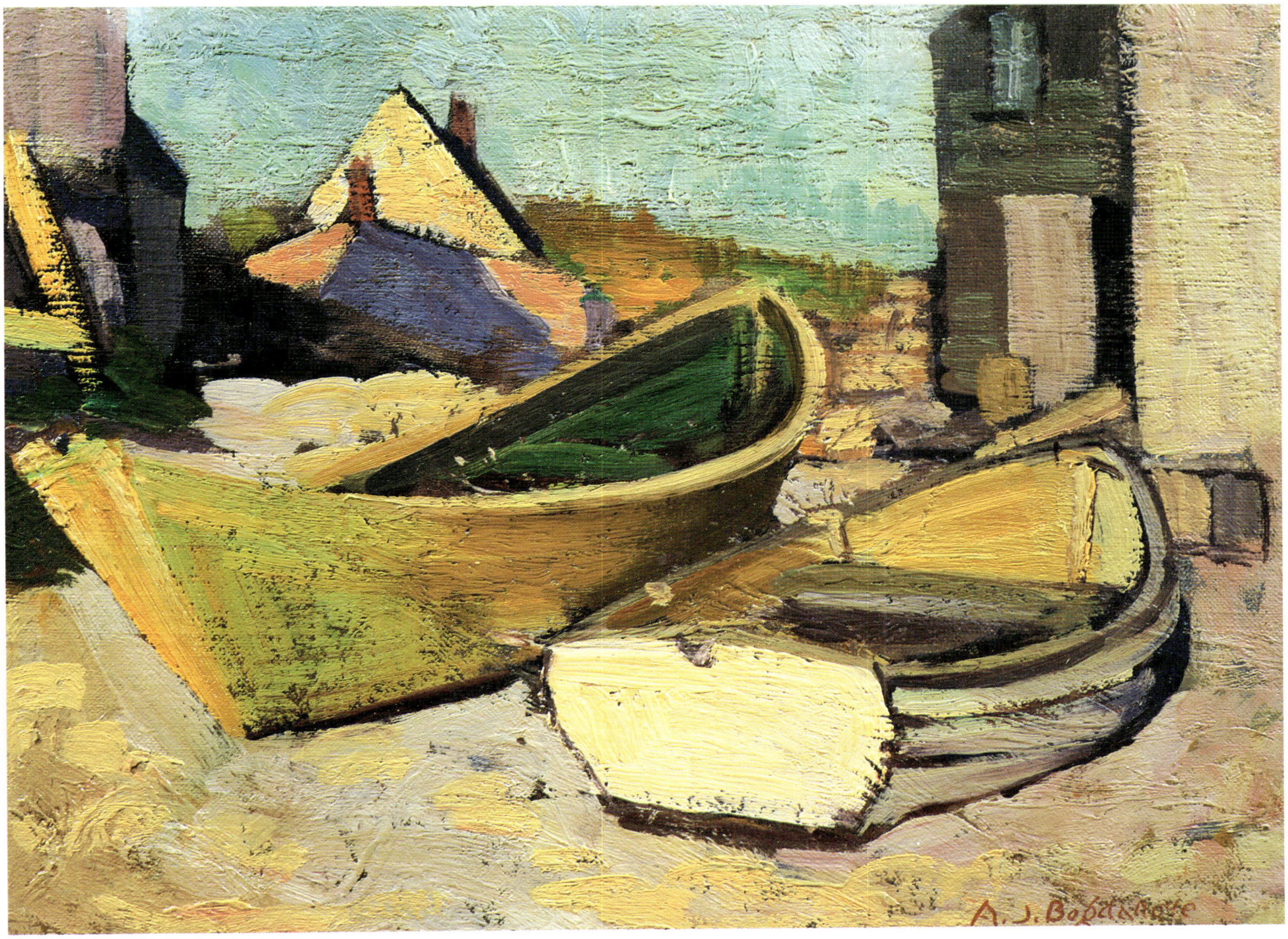
A. J. Bogdanove

38.

The Gully, ca. 1930–1940

Oil on canvas
25 × 30 in. (63.5 × 76.2 cm)
Signed lower left: *A. J. Bogdanove*
Inscribed on stretcher: *The Gulley* [sic]

For Bogdanove, the rocks of Monhegan were ceaselessly interesting because of their many and constantly changing colors. In *The Gully,* he captured this facet of the island, conveying the impact of a stream of sunlight casting dappled reflections on a rocky chasm. Such imagery allowed him to explore the color theories of Maximilian Toch, a paint chemist for whom Bogdanove once worked. Toch asserted that colors are found in nature in perfect harmony and balance, a principle that Bogdanove conveyed in his variegated studies of Monhegan's scenery.

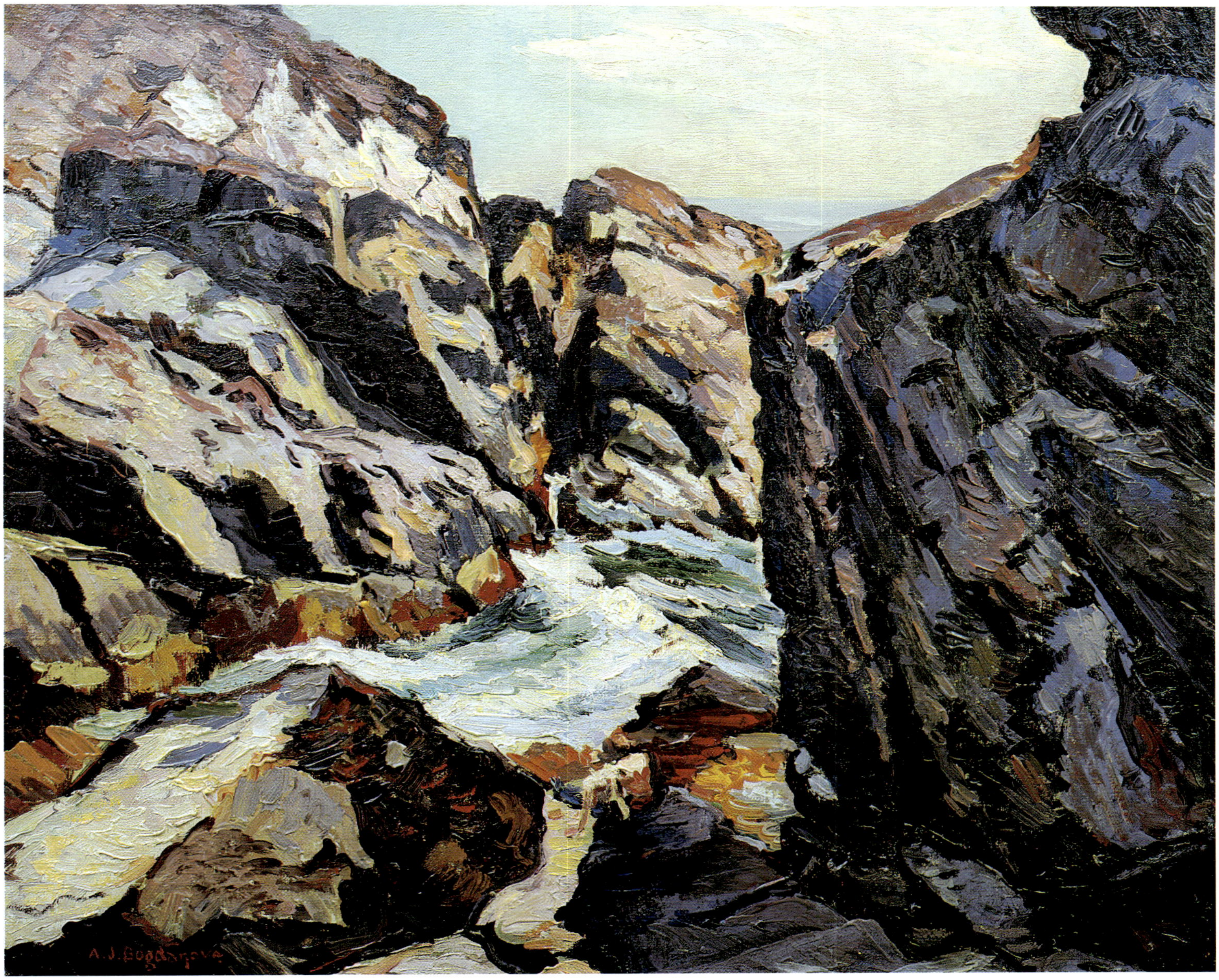
A.J. Bogdanova

39.

Dwight's Fish House, ca. 1930–1940

Oil on masonite
8⅞ × 11⅞ in. (22.4 × 30 cm)
Signed lower right: *A. J. Bogdanove*
Inscribed on verso: *Dwight's Fish House*

Dwight's Fish House, named for its owner Dwight Stanley, is a Monhegan landmark. Located on Fish Beach, one of two beaches on the harbor, the fish house still stands; in Bogdanove's time, its lower floor served as bait storage with an informal social club upstairs where fishermen and other locals gathered. The fish house has long been a favorite subject for artists, and Bogdanove was among those who saw the charm of the humble shack with its dense stacks of lobster pots lined up along its outer walls.

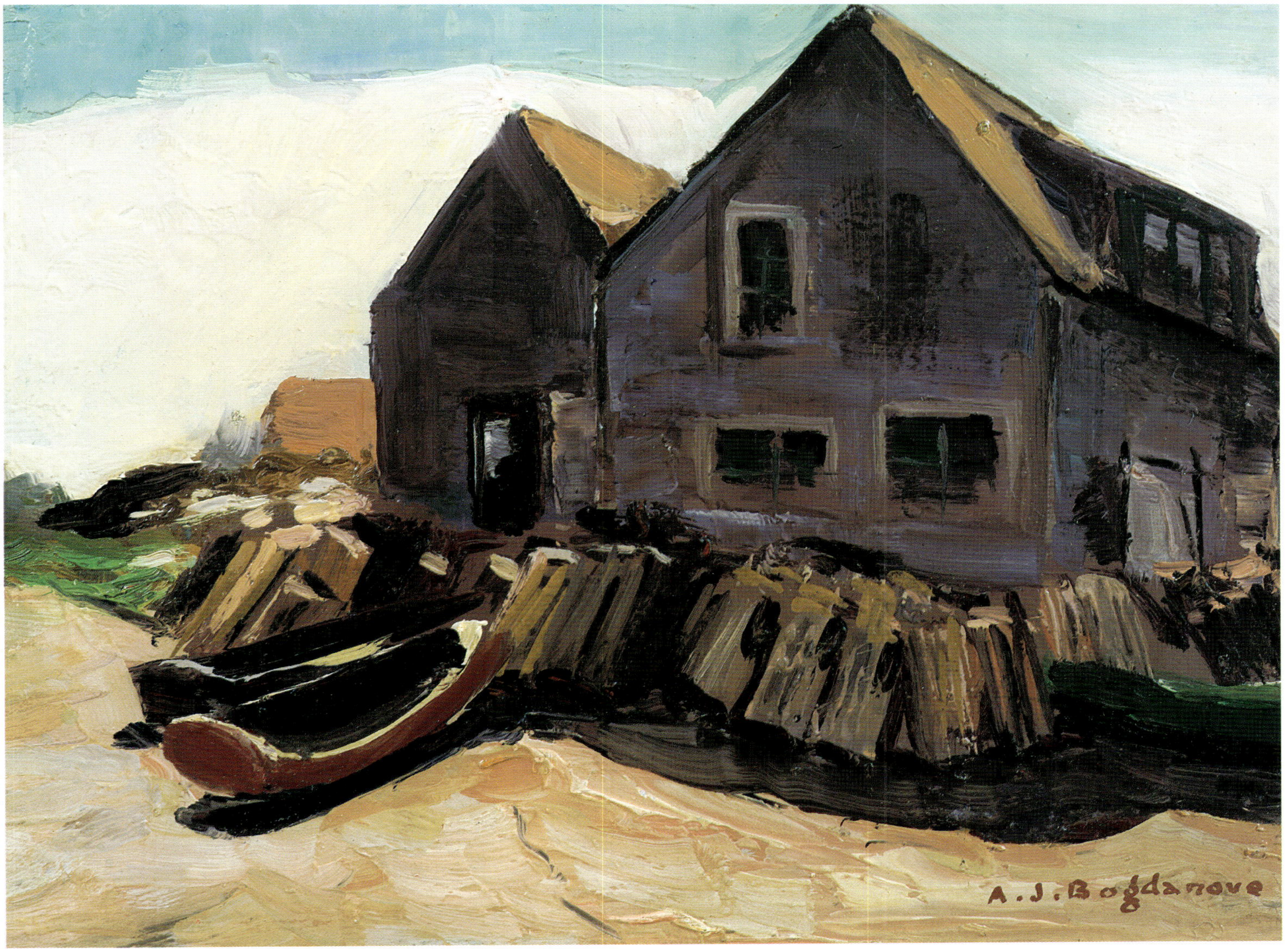
A.J.Bogdanove

40.

Lovely Day, ca. 1930–1935

Oil on canvas
25 × 30 in. (63.5 × 76.2 cm)
Inscribed on verso: *Lovely Day*

In *Lovely Day,* Bogdanove cropped his composition tightly, featuring a rocky mass that projects into the sea. Painting directly in the open air, he captured the blend of lavender and mauve reflections cast by the diffused sunlight on the broken surfaces of the rocks, creating a work that may be read equally in realistic and abstract terms.

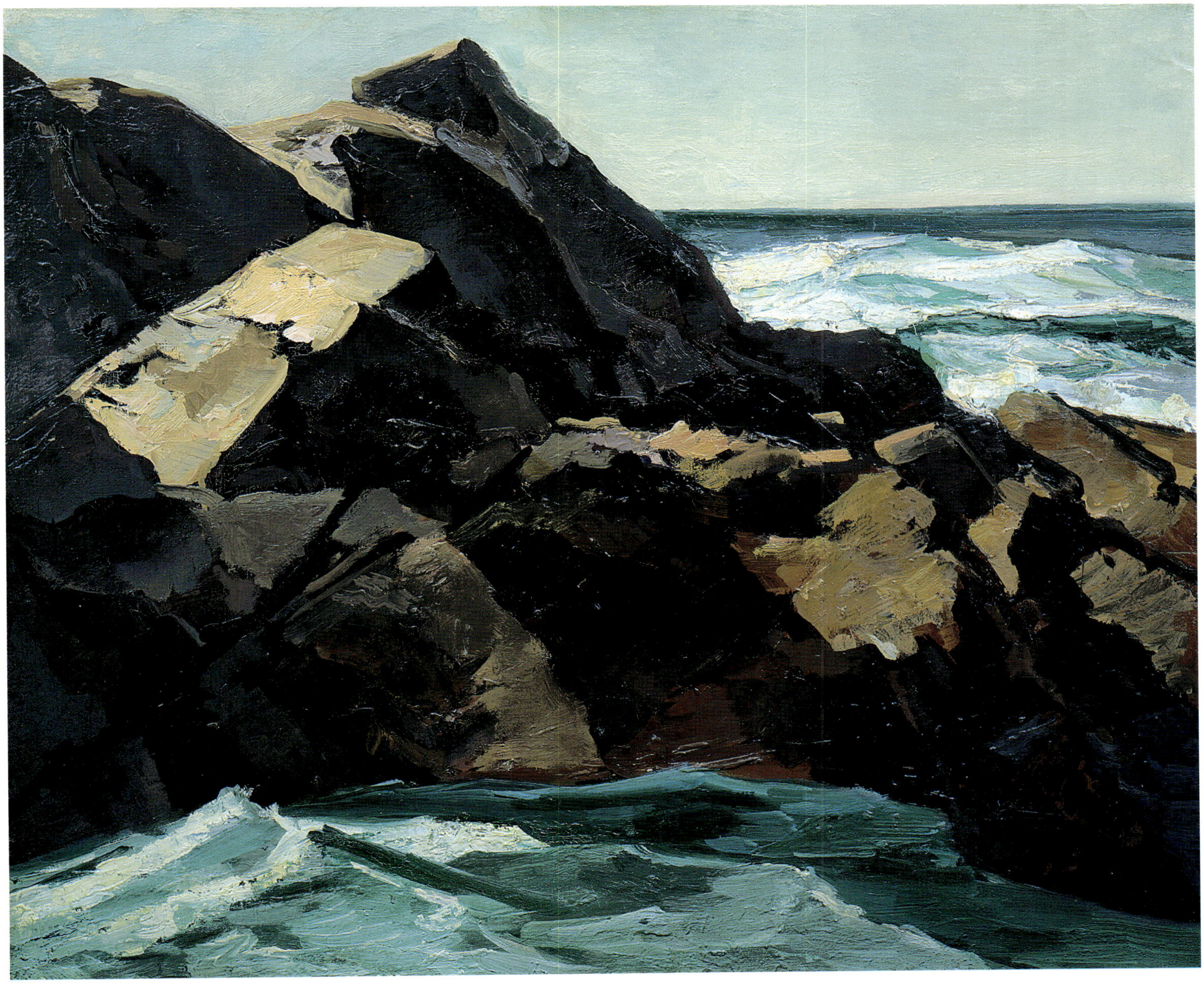

41.

Booth Bay Dock, ca. 1935–1940

Oil on canvasboard
20 × 24 in. (50.8 × 61 cm)
Inscribed on verso: *Booth Bay Dock*

The bustling seaside resort town of Boothbay Harbor, Maine, is an embarkation point for the seventeen-mile voyage to Monhegan Island. Boothbay's quaint commercial center and the manicured homes which surround it stand in sharp contrast to Monhegan's rusticity. It is possible that Bogdanove created his briskly painted *Booth Bay Dock,* a view of a weathered pier and fishing shack, while waiting for the "Monhegan boat," as the ferry to the island is called.

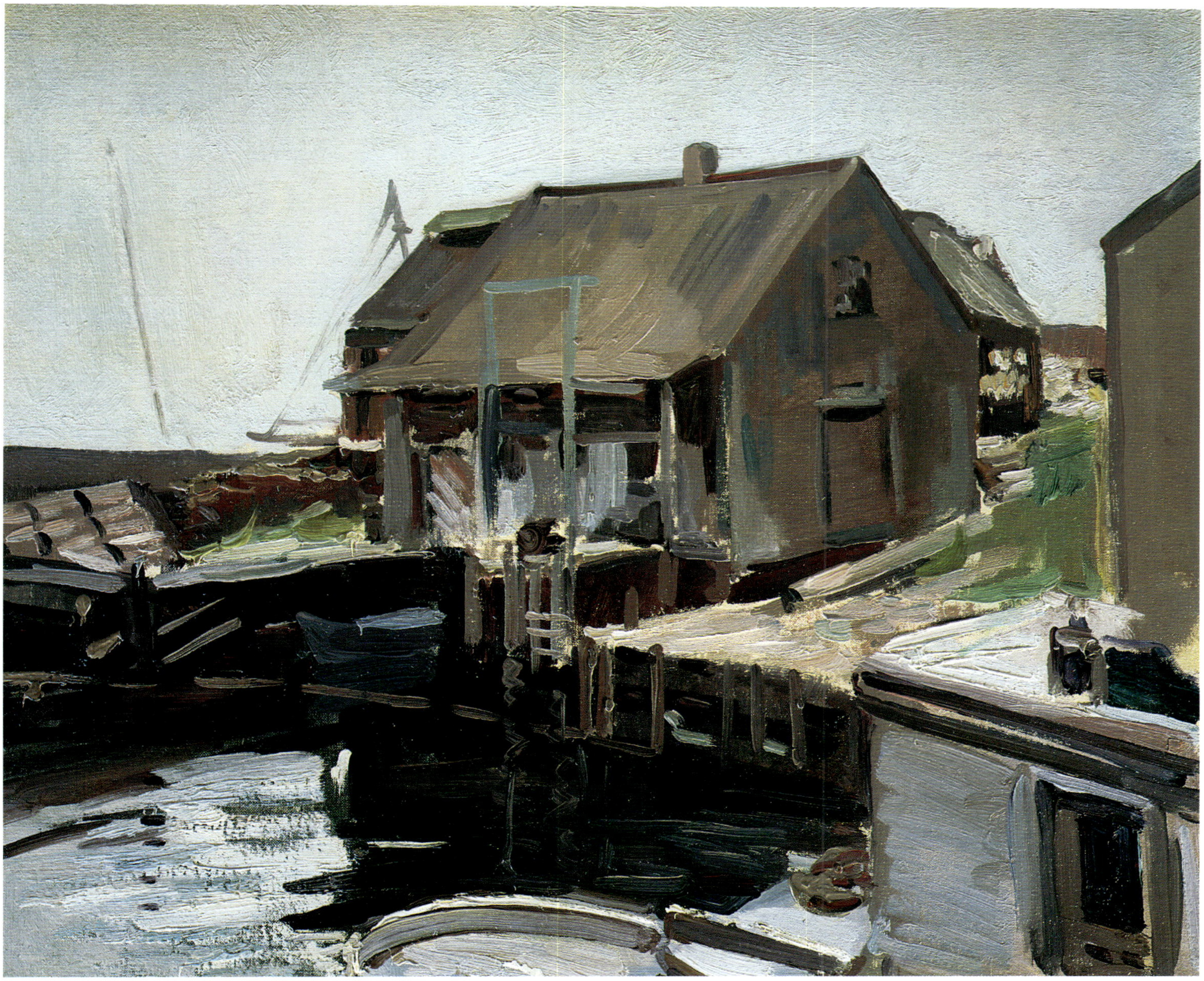

42.

Marine, ca. 1918–1928

Oil on board

8 × 10 in. (20.3 × 25.4 cm)

Signed indistinctly lower right: *A. J. Bogdanove*

Inscribed on verso: *Marine*

Marine is typical of the *pochades* (small, quick sketches) that Bogdanove executed from nature. Working directly, Bogdanove applied slashing strokes of unmixed color to capture the energy of the sea, a method akin to that of Robert Henri. Neither artist prepared *pochades* with the traditional intention of using them as studies for studio paintings; rather, both saw them as complete statements that conveyed immediate impressions of specific moments.

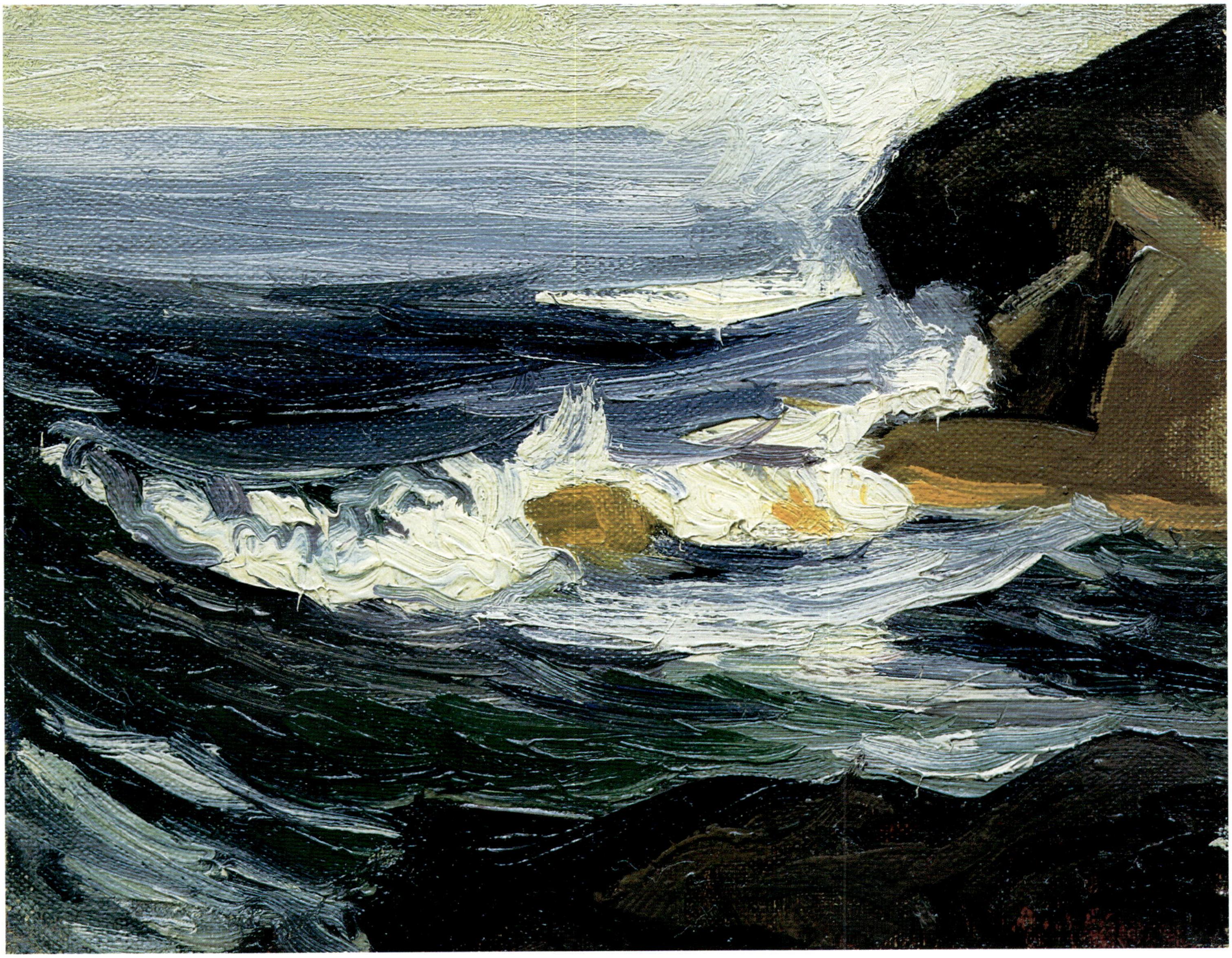

43.

Fish Shack and Lobster Pots, ca. 1925–1935

Oil on canvas
25 × 30 in. (63.5 × 76.2 cm)

Fish Shack and Lobster Pots portrays Dwight Stanley's fish house, one of Monhegan's most frequently painted subjects. In the work, Bogdanove captured the picturesque qualities of such unassuming elements as weathered siding, a ramp, and lobster buoys, which hang beside the door. Indeed, Bogdanove was among the first painters on Monhegan to depict this fish house as a classic icon of the island.

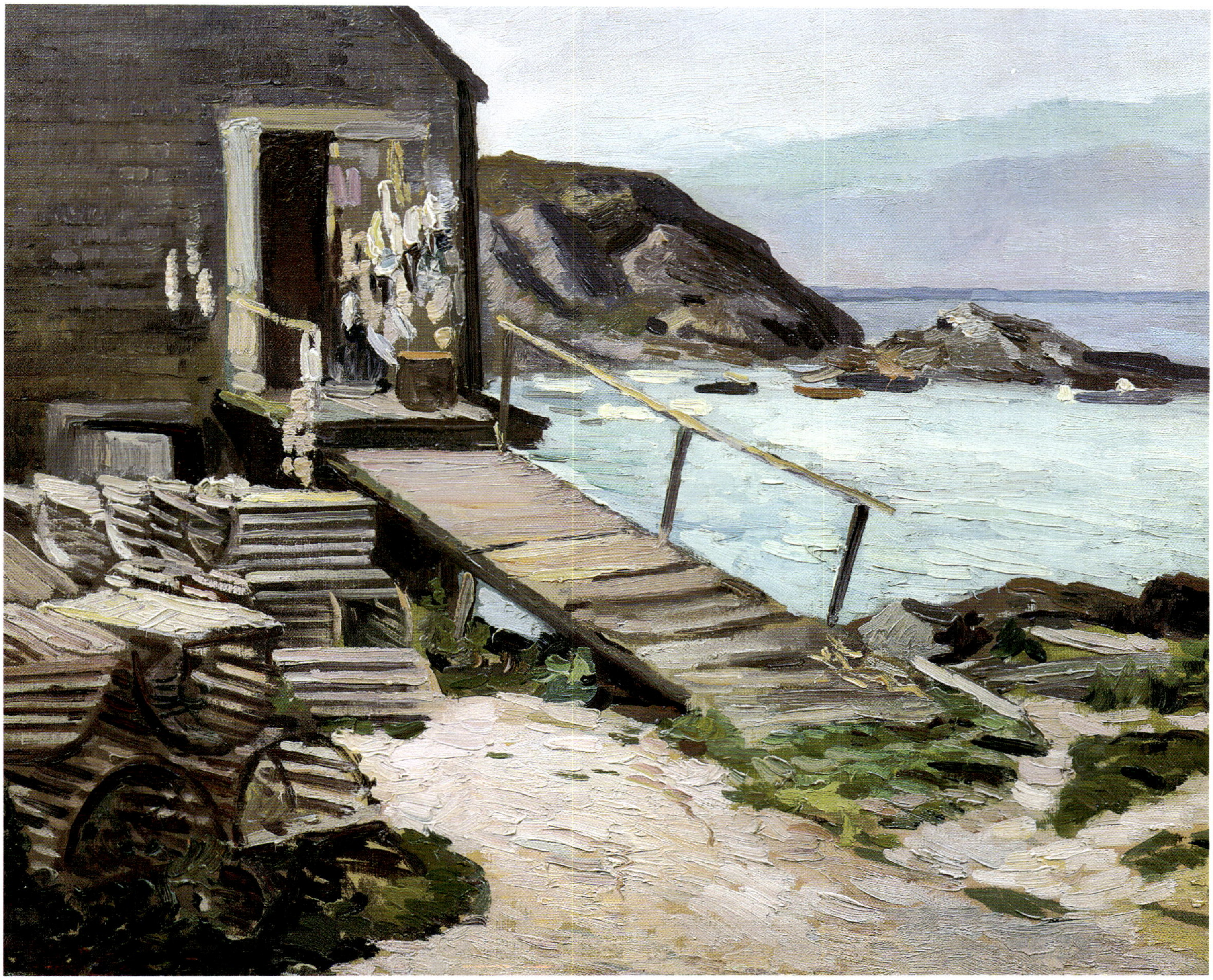

44.

Landscape by the Sea, ca. 1912–1917

Oil on canvas
25 × 29⅞ in. (63.5 × 75.8 cm)
Signed lower left: *A. J. Bogdanove*

The site depicted in this landscape has yet to be identified. However, since the painting demonstrates the quick, Impressionist brushwork typical of Bogdanove's landscapes of the 1910s, it may have been executed in New Jersey or Connecticut, where the artist often painted during this decade. The work is characteristic of Bogdanove's art at a time when he was breaking away from the crisp brushwork and academic approach he employed in his murals.

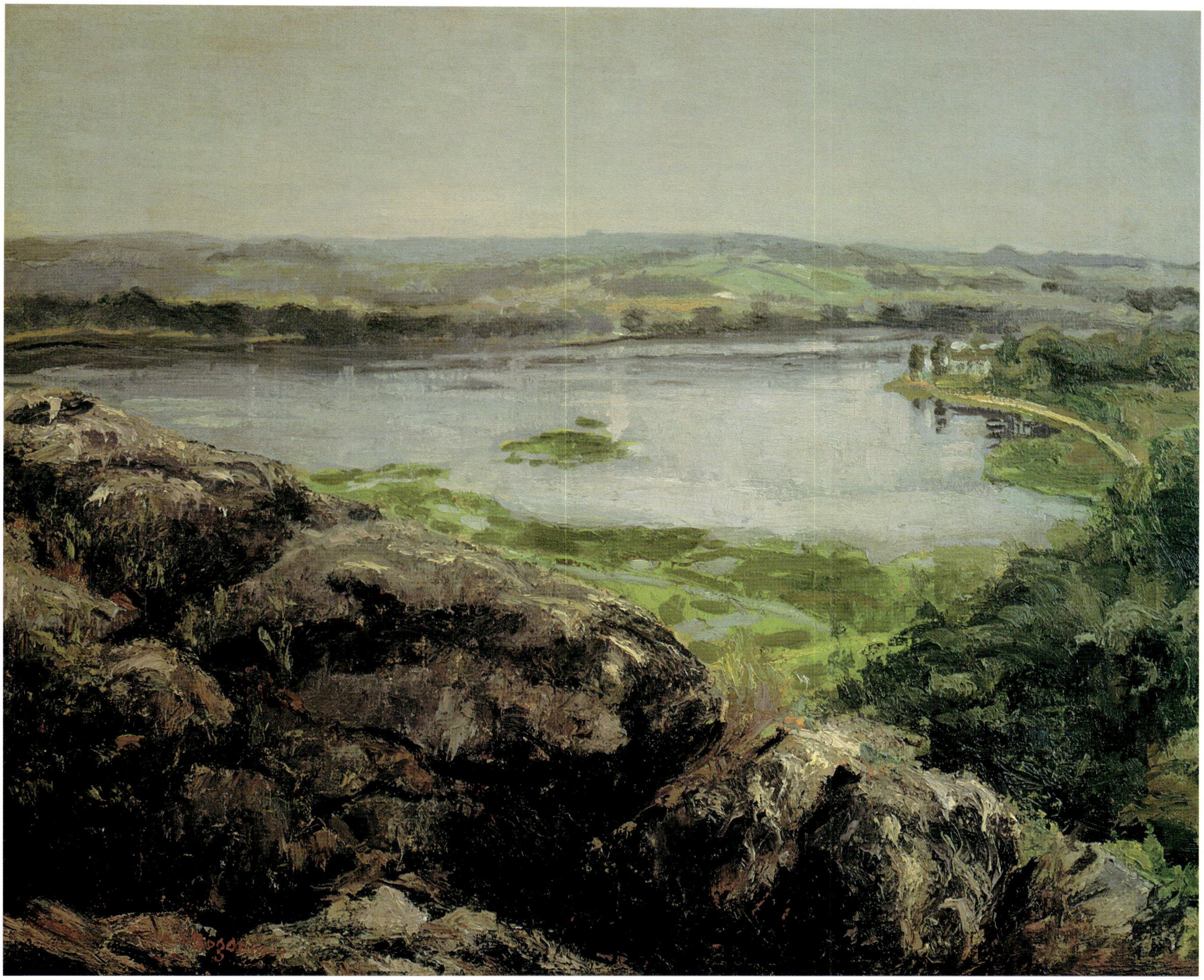

45.

Seaside Village, ca. 1918–1925

Oil on canvas
30 × 35½ in. (76.2 × 90.2 cm)

Seaside Village depicts a cluster of buildings on Monhegan Island, seen against the shadowy mass of neighboring Manana Island. Bogdanove used a similar palette and brushwork in *Creek Woods, Connecticut,* executed in 1914 (pl. 15), which suggests that *Seaside Village* was painted during one of Bogdanove's first stays on Monhegan. While sunlight fills the foreground, where a group of homes are situated, a mist has settled over the sea. Such conditions, which are typical on Monhegan, reveal the magical experience offered by a stay on the island.

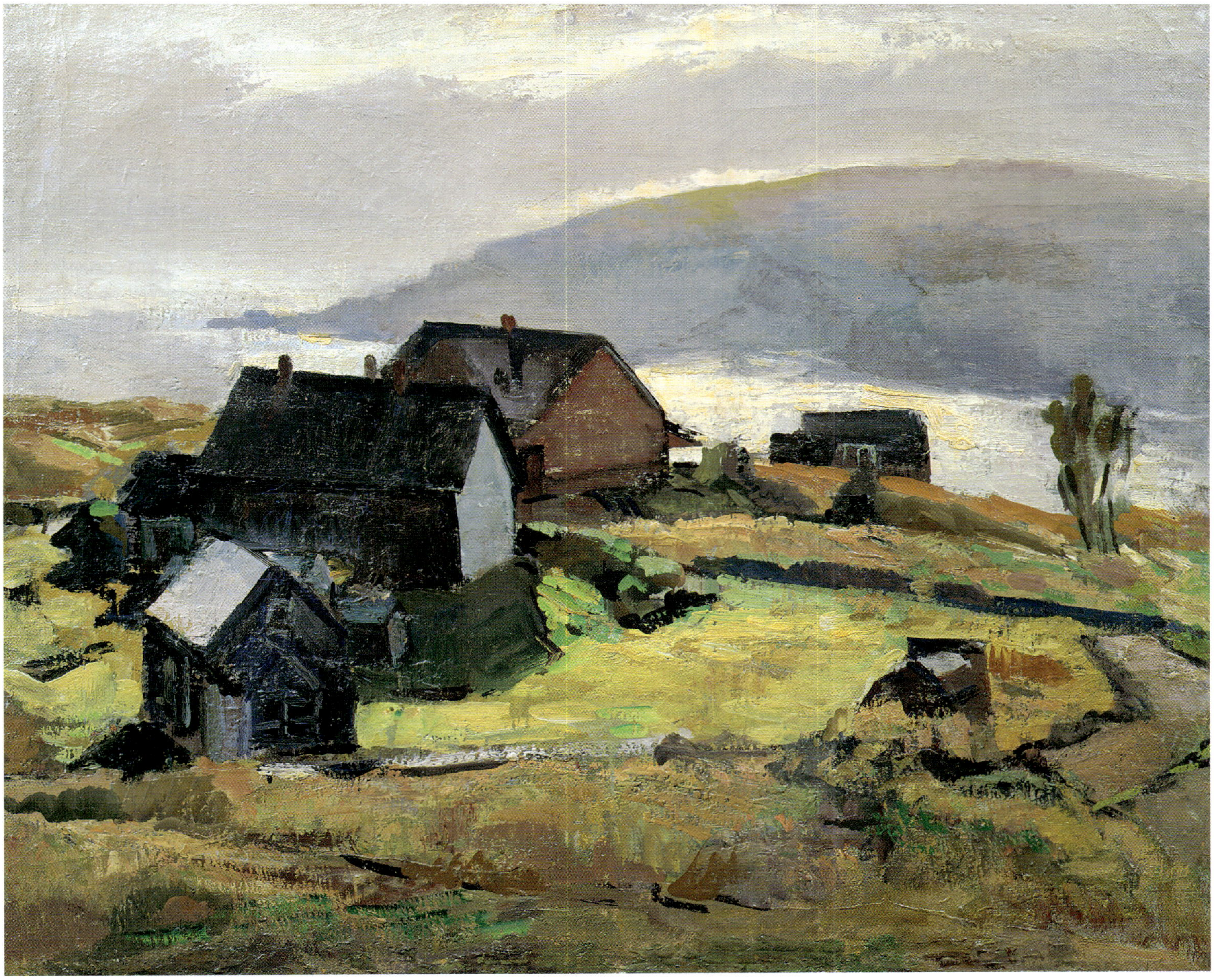

46.

The Red House, ca. 1910–1920

Oil on board
7⅞ × 12 in. (19.9 × 30.5 cm)
Signed lower right: *A. J. Bogdanove*

Bogdanove probably painted *The Red House* on one of the forays he took to Maine, New Jersey, and Connecticut in the 1910s. While the painting is executed in the Impressionist style typical of Bogdanove's early work, it also shows the interest in color relationships that would emerge in his mature art. Here, subtly varying greens offset the rust-red tone of the house, accentuating its vibrancy.

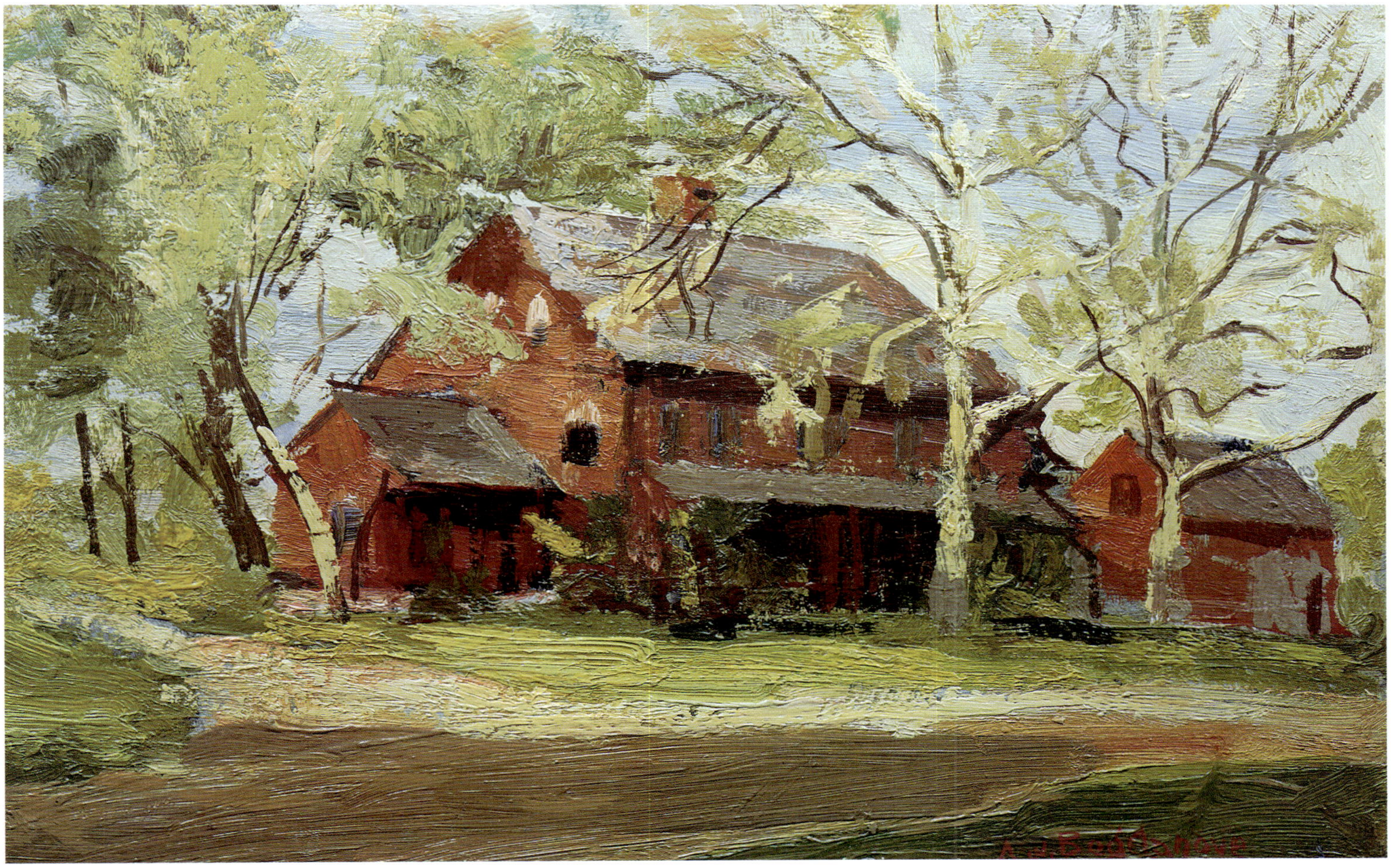

47.

Fisherman's House, ca. 1930–1940

Oil on board
20 × 24 in. (50.8 × 61 cm)
Signed lower right: *A. J. Bogdanove*

Current residents of Monhegan Island still recall seeing Bogdanove standing during many mornings at the water's edge painting images of the harbor, its boats and fish houses. Indeed, Monhegan's harbor, seen from the beach, was one of Bogdanove's favorite views. In images of this subject including *Drydock* (pl. 8), *Boat and Boathouse* (pl. 33), and *Fisherman's House,* the artist featured the same weathered building, capturing the contrast between the play of sunlight on the near shore and the dark land masses that stretch across the horizon in the distance.

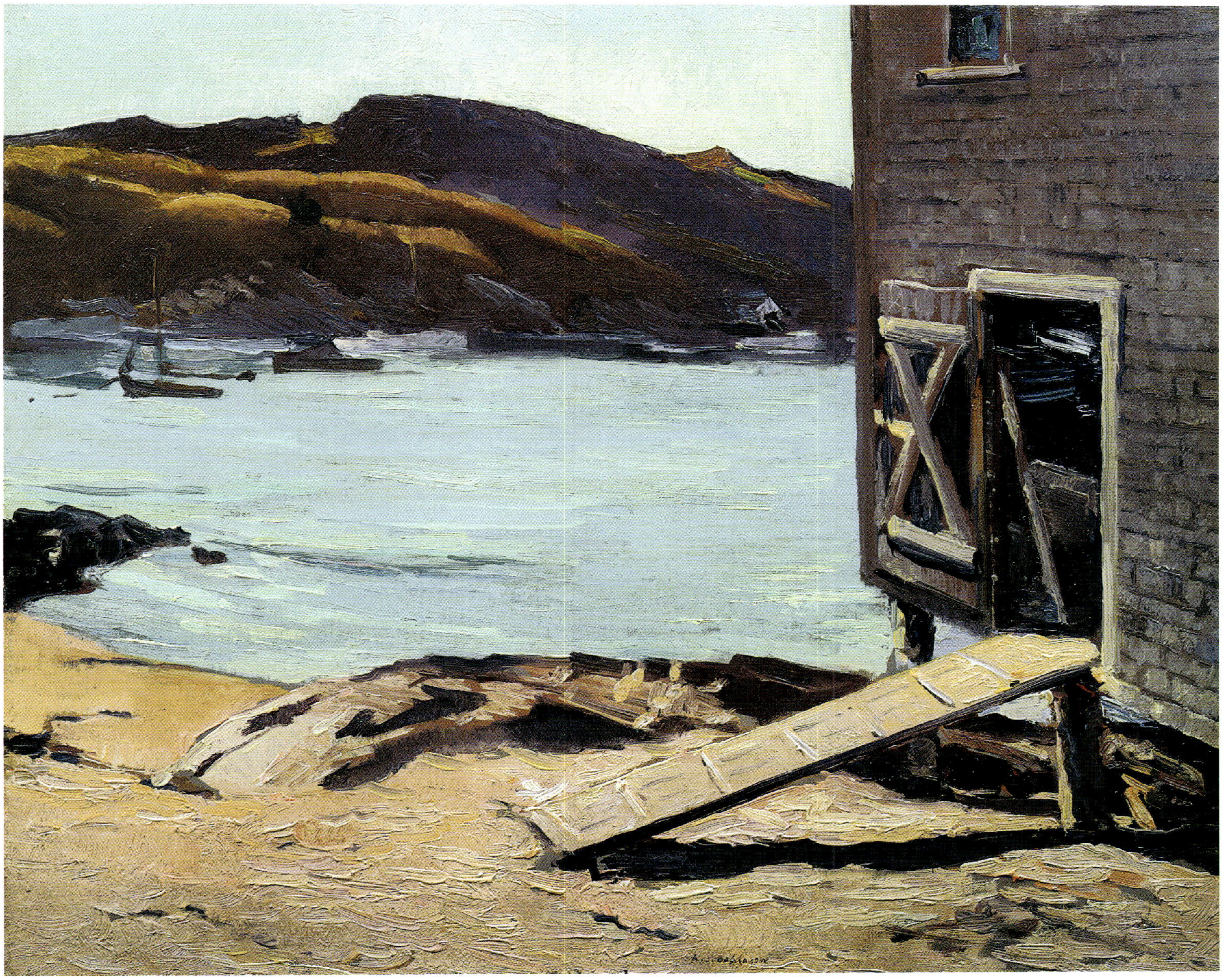

48.

Wrestlers, ca. 1940–1943

Oil on canvas

30 × 36 in. (76.2 × 91.4 cm)

In the early 1940s, Bogdanove created a series of paintings of wrestlers. Executed during the winters in his New York City studio, these works reveal a different dimension of his output. As in the boxing paintings of George Bellows, Bogdanove captured the gritty nature of the sport and the generalized faces of spectators who crowd around the ring. This painting is possibly the work titled *The Headlock,* which was shown in the 1943 winter annual exhibition at the National Academy of Design and in Bogdanove's 1961 memorial exhibition at The College of The City of New York.

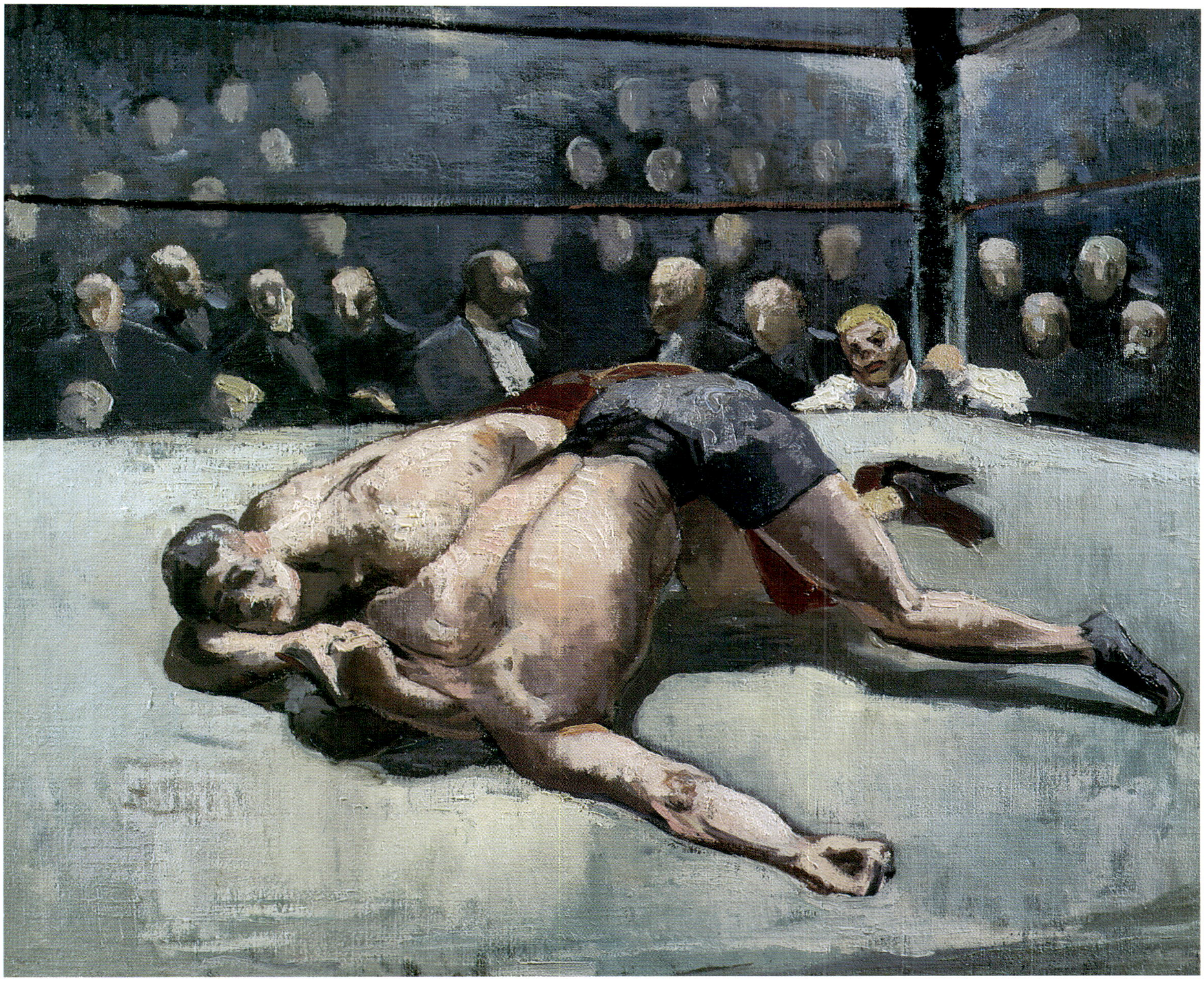

Chronology

1886
Born Minsk, Russia, probably on September 2

1890s
Attends the Reale Schule, Minsk

1900
Emigrates with his family to New York City

1900–1903
Studies at Cooper Union Institute of Art in New York

1903
Serves as an apprentice painting advertisement displays for the Bull Durham Company in New York
Enters National Academy of Design School where he studies with George W. Maynard and Francis Coates Jones through 1911

ca. 1903–1908
Works as a draftsman for the *New York Journal*, where he meets Mark Twain

1908–1910
Studies at Columbia University School of Architecture, New York

1909
Receives National Academy of Design Cannon Prize for painting from the nude
Receives National Academy of Design second Hallgarten Prize for painting

1910
Receives National Academy of Design first Hallgarten Prize for painting
Receives National Academy of Design first prize for sculpture

1910–1916
Paints in Leonia, New Jersey

1911
Receives National Academy of Design first Hallgarten Prize for painting

1912
Travels to Italy, Germany, Austria, and France
First mural commission, for the Hebrew Sheltering and Guardian Society, Pleasantville, New York

1913
Receives a license from New York City Board of Education as a specialist in mural decoration
Teaches at the New York Evening School of Industrial Art until 1939
Strong Faith (*The Sacrifice*), a mural study, shown in the twenty-eighth annual exhibition of the Architectural League of New York

1915–1917
Summers at Seal Harbor, Mount Desert Island, Maine

1917
Becomes a member of the Society of Independent Artists

1918
First visits Monhegan Island
Participates in *Exhibition of Paintings*, the MacDowell Club, New York, October 15–27
Completes two murals, *Ancient Commerce* and *Modern Commerce*, in the auditorium of the Commercial High School, Brooklyn (unveiled November 19)

1919
Teaches art at Townsend Harris High School of the College of the City of New York (now City College of The City University of New York), continues until 1942

1920
Purchases a house / studio on Horn's Hill, Monhegan, Maine
Exhibition of Paintings by A. J. Bogdanove, held at the Young Men's Hebrew Association, New York (April 17 – May 22)

ca. 1920
Marries Pearl Winton, former student

1922
Peace mural completed in the main stairway at the Manual Training High School, Brooklyn (dedicated November 7 in memory of the twenty-five school graduates who died serving in World War I)

1923–1924
Teaches art at the College of the City of New York

1924–1925
Teaches for the Rehabilitation of War Veterans Bureau

1925
Son Emanuel (Mendel) born
Exhibition of twenty-eight marines held at the City Club of New York (November)
Completes *Wisdom Giveth Life* for the main entrance of Commercial High School, Brooklyn

1926
Completes *The Arrival of the Mayflower* mural for Public School 43 in The Bronx

1928
Son Nathaniel (Tanny) born

1929
Paintings by A. J. Bogdanove, held at the Clayton Gallery, New York (October)

1930
Has one-man exhibition at the Lamson & Hubbard Gallery, Boston (November)
Completes *The Caravels of Columbus* mural for Public School 43 in The Bronx
Completes *The Great Teachers* mural in Shepherd Hall, College of the City of New York

1934
Becomes a member of the Salmagundi Club, New York

1935
Travels to Gaspé Peninsula, Canada; sketches cliffs and fishing villages

1936
Recent Marine Paintings of the Coast of Maine held at The Leonard Clayton Gallery, New York (April)

1938
Travels to Europe, where he visits museums in Italy, Spain, France, Holland, and Great Britain and sketches in Normandy, France, and on the Cornwall coast in England

1941
Receives the James B. Carrington Prize at the annual oil exhibition at the Salmagundi Club (February 9–28) for *Turtle Rock, Monhegan*

1942
Receives award for *Ground Swell* at the twenty-ninth annual exhibition of the Allied American Artists, New York
Retires from teaching position at Townsend Harris High School of the College of the City of New York
Moves to Dunbarton, New Hampshire

1946
Dies in August in Dunbarton, New Hampshire

1957
Paintings of the Maine Coast and Other Oils held at the Farnsworth Museum, Rockland, Maine (November 22 – December 29)

1961
A. J. Bogdanove Memorial Exhibit held at the College of the City of New York (February 9 – March 9)

1965
Paintings by A.J. Bogdanove held at the Incurable Collector, New York (May 5–25)

Index of Illustrations

Unless otherwise indicated, all works by Abraham J. Bogdanove featured in this catalogue are from the estate of the artist.

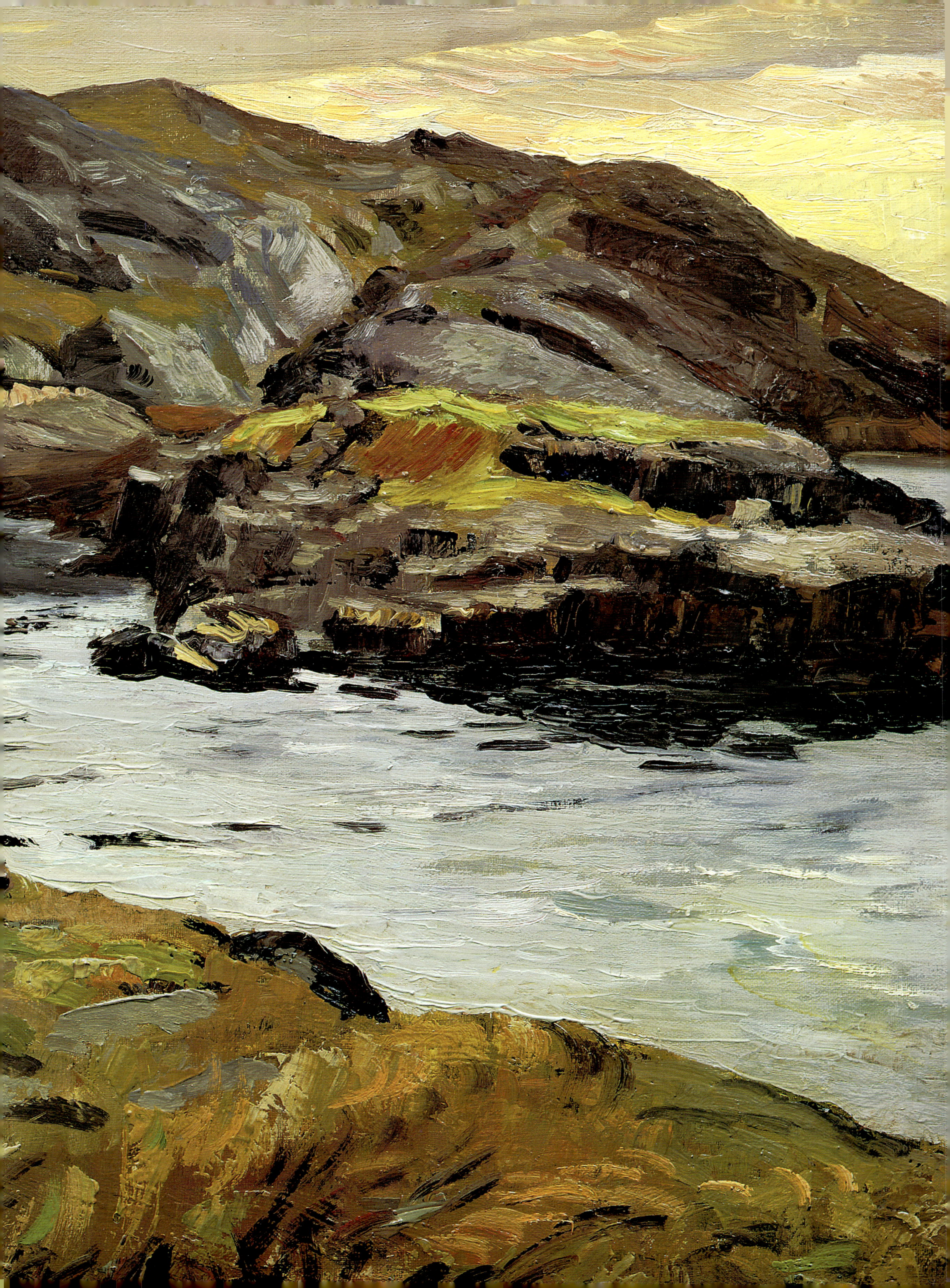

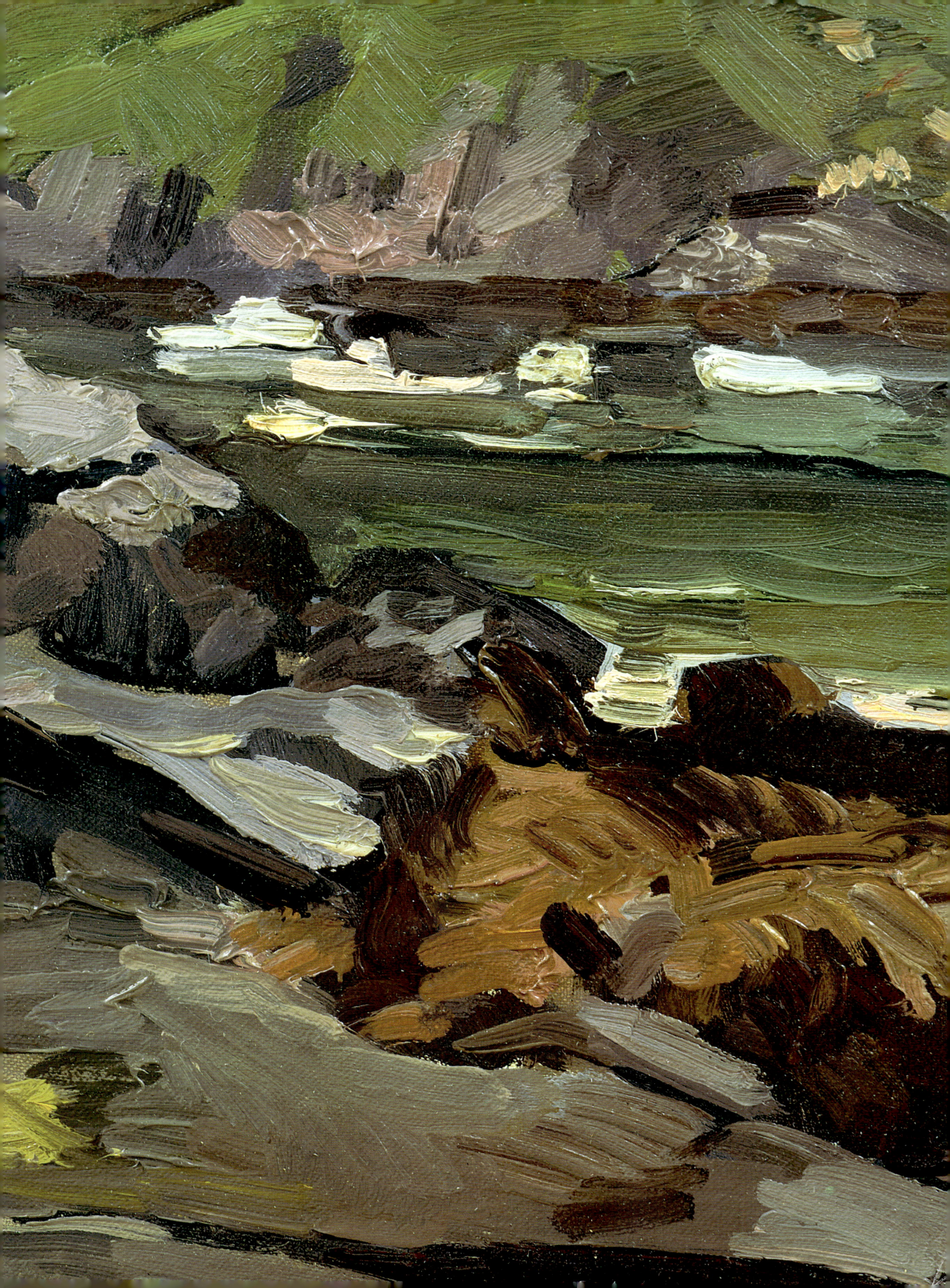

PRESS RELEASE

Spanierman Gallery, LLC
45 East 58th Street New York, NY 10022-1617
Telephone (212) 832-0208 Fax (212) 832-8114

FOR IMMEDIATE RELEASE
Contact: Ira Spanierman or Deborah Gerstler Spanierman

Abraham J. Bogdanove (1886–1946): Painter of Maine

July 28 through September 27, 1997

Web-Site: http://www.Spanierman.com
E-mail address: Info@Spanierman.com
Gallery Hours: Monday through Saturday 9:30 to 5:30

Spanierman Gallery is pleased to announce the opening on July 28, 1997 of *Abraham J. Bogdanove (1886–1946): Painter of Maine*. This exhibition showcases the work of Abraham Bogdanove, a landscape painter, portraitist, muralist, and art teacher, who is best known for his dynamic images of Monhegan Island, Maine. Including forty-nine works, this is the first major exhibition of Bogdanove's work since the artist's memorial show in 1961 at the College of The City of New York (now City College of The City University of New York). Accompanying the show is a fully illustrated scholarly catalogue by Jessica Nicoll, chief curator at the Portland Museum of Art, Maine, which may be purchased from the gallery.

Like Robert Henri and Edward Hopper, Bogdanove was inspired by the stark drama of Monhegan Island. Returning there every summer from 1918 until the end of his life, he spent his days hiking onto the rocky outcroppings at the water's edge, where he applied energetic brushstrokes with vigor and gusto to capture the ever-changing coloristic and compositional possibilities of crashing waves and jagged rocks. Whereas other artists saw only gray tones in Monhegan's rocks, Bogdanove perceived them to be full of color, and he captured their vivacity with a wide-ranging palette. He also chronicled Monhegan's harbor and fish houses, demonstrating an attention to the form-defining properties of light that parallel Hopper's. While Bogdanove captured the animated qualities of his subject matter, he also created strong, abstract designs that reflect his understanding of modernist principles.

Born in Minsk, Russia, Bogdanove emigrated with his family to New York City in 1900. Immediately following his arrival in America, he began to study art, enrolling at the Cooper Union Institute of Art, the National Academy of Design, and the Columbia University School of Architecture. At Columbia, Bogdanove trained with the important muralist Francis Millet, who inspired him to explore this genre for himself. By 1912, Bogdanove had begun to receive commissions for murals in which he addressed historical, educational, or moral themes and presented images in simple and graphic terms so that they could be quickly comprehended. His last mural, *The Great Teachers*, 1930, may today be found in Shepherd Hall at City College of The City of New York.

(over)

As he realized his aspirations as a muralist, Bogdanove increasingly devoted his free time, particularly the summers, to painting for himself. While his first paintings were allied to his murals, demonstrating academic styles and didactic messages, by the 1910s, he had begun to visit the countrysides of Connecticut and New Jersey, and to paint the landscapes he observed directly in a lively Impressionist style. In search of new subject matter, Bogdanove traveled to Maine for the first time in the summer of 1915. Staying at Seal Harbor on Mount Desert Island, he painted the dramatic vistas of mountains plunging to the sea that had previously fascinated the Hudson River School painter Frederic Edwin Church and the Luminist Fitz Hugh Lane.

However, for Bogdanove, the refinements of summer life on Mount Desert had lost their attraction by 1918, and his desire for a rougher locale was satisfied by Monhegan, a tiny island seventeen miles off Maine's midcoast. Instead of mountainous scenery, Monhegan offered a compact and varied landscape, unique among the hundreds of islands that dot Maine's waters. Less than two miles long and a mile wide, the island includes a picturesque harbor lined with fish houses, rolling meadows, pine woods, and cliffs soaring two hundred feet above the ocean. A contrast to the more accessible, tamer summer resorts like Gloucester, Massachusetts, and Ogunquit, Maine, Monhegan is remote and quiet, and its immense rocks and turbulent surf offer a wide variety of inspirational subject matter. Among the first artists to visit Monhegan, Henri declared that he had "never seen anything so fine" and stated: "It is a wonderful place to paint—so much in so small a place one can hardly believe it."

Bogdanove may well have known Henri's Monhegan images, as well as those of John Sloan, George Bellows, and Rockwell Kent. Indeed, his method of painting directly on panels fitted into the lid of his paint box parallels that of Henri. Bogdanove's frequent use of vibrant yellows, oranges, and blues evokes Kent's style, while the physical strength of his brushwork is similar to that of Bellows. Bogdanove may also have drawn on his knowledge of the seascapes of Winslow Homer, who had portrayed wrathful waves assaulting leaden rocks while living at Prout's Neck, Maine, at the turn of the twentieth century. In a number of works, Bogdanove used Homer's strategy of conveying the force of the sea and the resistance of rocks by positioning the viewer at a low vantage point behind rocks, directly confronting a pounding wave.

Bogdanove had begun to receive renown for his Monhegan views by 1920, when his first solo exhibition was held at the Young Men's Hebrew Association in New York. Shortly thereafter, his Maine images began to be shown at annual exhibitions at such institutions as the National Academy of Design, the Pennsylvania Academy of the Fine Arts, and the Carnegie Institute. In 1930, an exhibition of Bogdanove's marines was held at the Lamson and Hubbard Gallery in Boston.

Over time, Bogdanove helped introduce Monhegan to a new generation of artists, and even today, the painters who gather on the island during the summer to portray its scenery carry on Bogdanove's legacy. Bold and peaceful, Bogdanove's Monhegan images are an evocation of their creator and speak to the special inspiration that the island offered, and continues to offer, to artists.

they have not really hurt the wild effect of the island except in the village part they have not added to its character or its beauty.

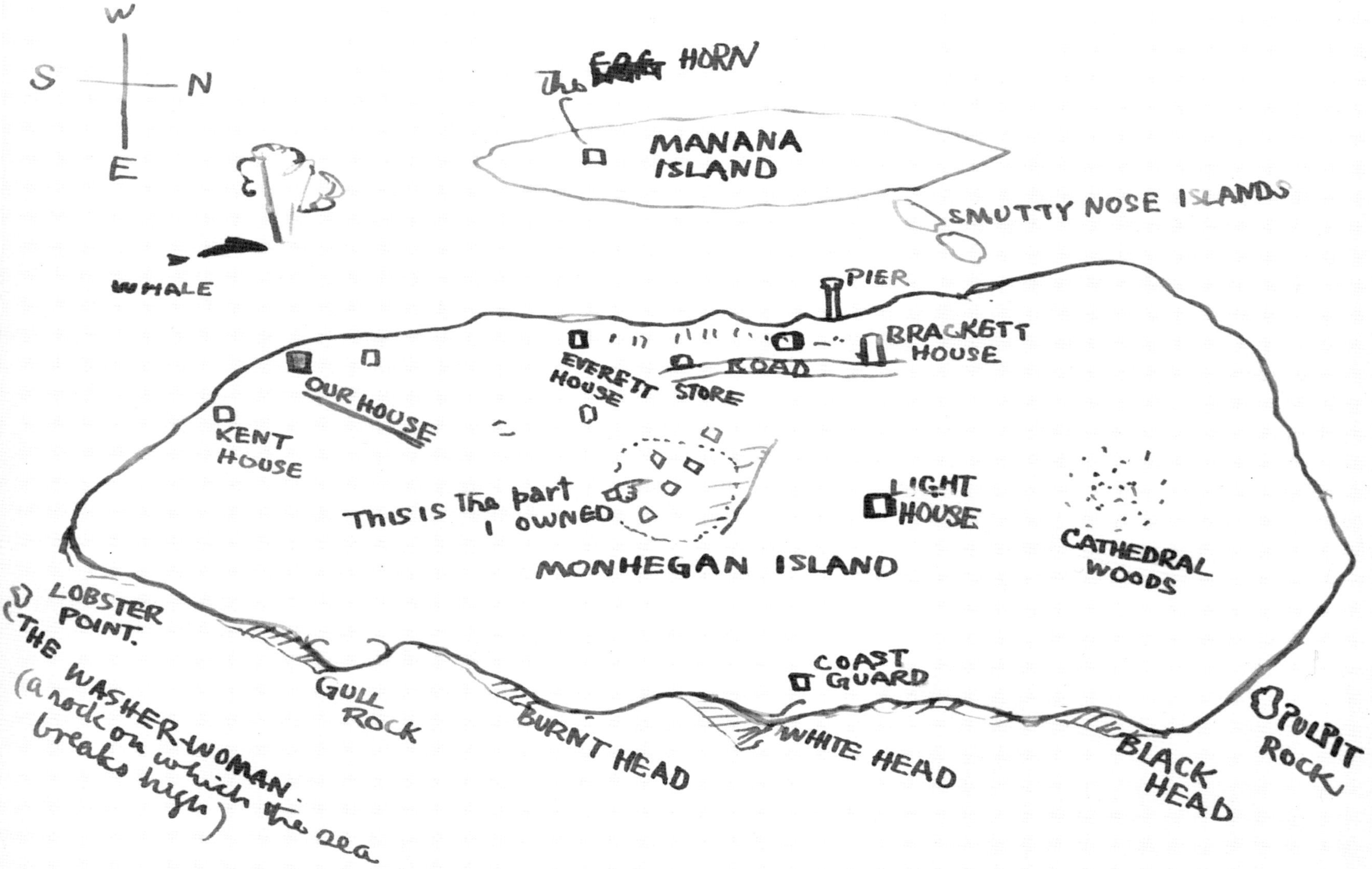

This is by no means a correct map but it will serve to recall to you the island and the lay of the land and will show you where our house is — note the red spot.

We met Everett last night. He does not seem much older. looks very much the same altho quite gray — white. He is the same enthusiast about art. is now the

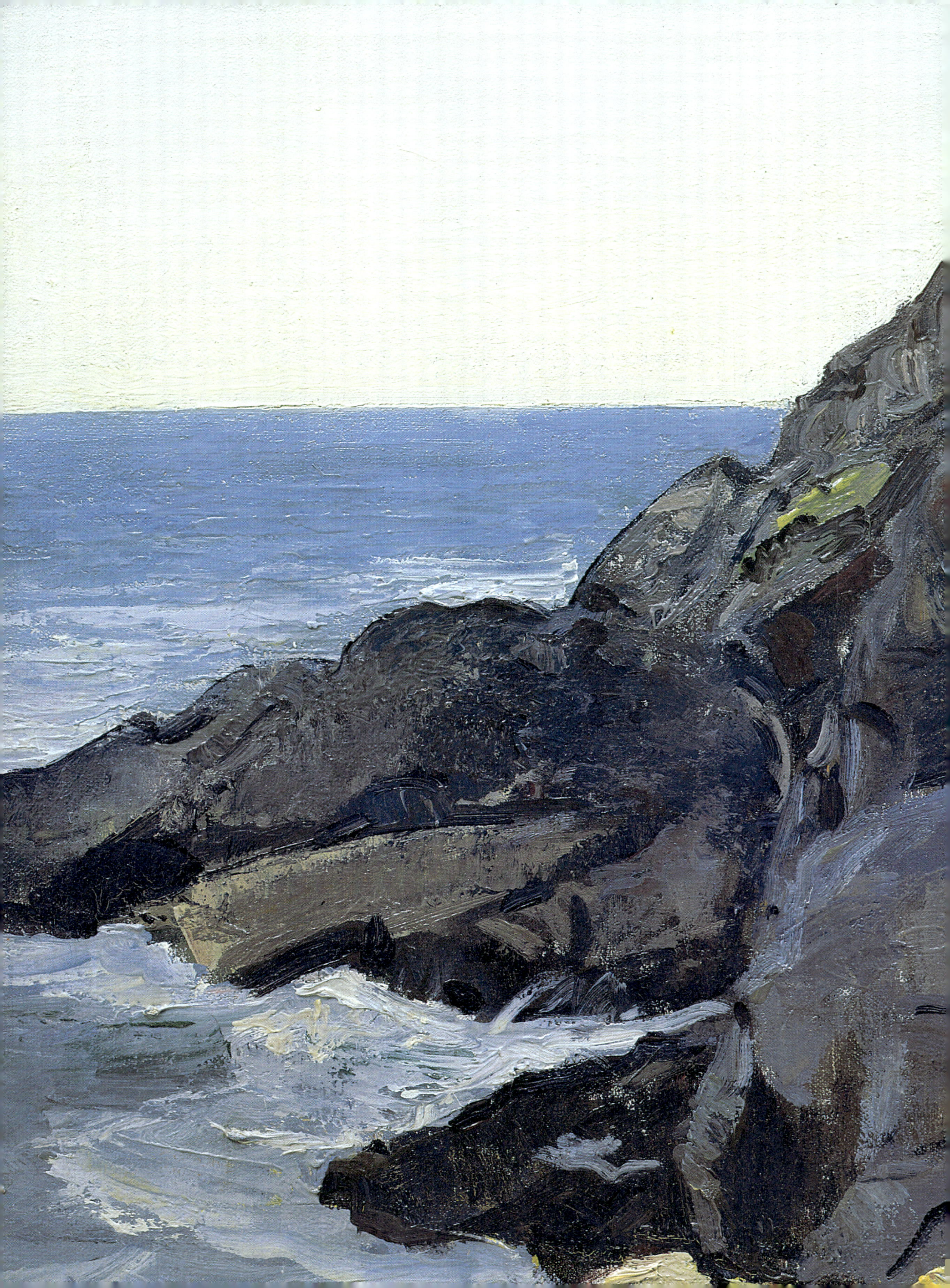